TECHNOLOGY FOR INCLUSION

FOURTH EDITION

TECHNOLOGY FOR INCLUSION

Meeting the Special Needs of All Students

MARY MALE

San Jose State University

Boston   New York   San Francisco
Mexico City   Montreal   Toronto   London   Madrid   Munich   Paris
Hong Kong   Singapore   Tokyo   Cape Town   Sydney

Vice President: *Paul A. Smith*
Executive Editor: *Virginia Lanigan*
Editorial Assistant: *Robert Champaigne*
Marketing Manager: *Amy Cronin*
Editorial Production Service: *Chestnut Hill Enterprises, Inc.*
Manufacturing Buyer: *JoAnne Sweeney*
Cover Administrator: *Kristina Mose-Libon*
Electronic Composition: *Omegatype Typography, Inc.*

For related titles and support material, visit our online catalogue at www.ablongman.com.

Between the time Website information is gathered and then published, it is not unusual for some sites to have closed. Also, the transcription of URLs can result in unintended typographical errors. The publisher would appreciate notification where these occur so that they may be corrected in subsequent editions.

Library of Congress Cataloging-in-Publication Data

Male, Mary.
    Technology for inclusion: meeting the special needs of all students / Mary Male. — 4th ed.
      p. cm.
    Includes bibliographical references and index.
    ISBN 0-205-34220-5
      1. Special education—United States—Computer-assisted instruction. 2. Special education—United States—Data processing. 3. Educational technology—United States.
    4. Inclusive education—United States. I. Title

LC3969.5 .M37 2003
371.9'0285–dc21
                                                           2002019378

Printed in the United States of America

10 9 8 7 6 5 4 3 2 1   07 06 05 04 03 02

CONTENTS

CHAPTER FOUR

Creating Catalysts for Social Growth: Cooperative Learning   29

CHAPTER FIVE

Technology across the Curriculum: Reading, Writing, Math, Science, and Social Studies   47

CHAPTER SIX

Designing Intensive Individual Interventions:
Disability-Specific Considerations   62

CHAPTER NINE

Creating Your Own Web Sites and Web Pages   103

CHAPTER TEN

Virtual Reality   115

CHAPTER ELEVEN
Technology and Service-Learning   122

CHAPTER TWELVE
Access   132

PREFACE

Each revision of this book has brought opportunities to reflect on both the magnitude of change in the field of special education and in technology and on the stability of the book's most powerful ideas. Students and their parents continue to press for access to technology that can expand opportunities for expression, communication, academic success, social participation, inclusion, and preparation for an independent life. Educators and service providers are energized by the experiences of their students and clients with technology and frustrated more than ever by funding shortage and bureaucratic barriers that delay meeting needs.

As with the earlier versions, ideas and examples for this book came from hundreds of hours of talking to students, parents, teachers, administrators, service providers, software and hardware designers, and professors who prepare special education personnel. Classroom observations, reviews of research, and pilot tests of lessons, software, and hardware with a wide range of students provided first-hand knowledge of what works, what doesn't, and why.

ACKNOWLEDGMENTS

I would like to thank students Amber Borgman and Susie Rigas, from San Jose State University and students from California State University, Chico, for their inspiration, dedication, curiosity, and commitment to making life better for their students that has guided the development of this book. Teachers from Chico who have contributed ideas and examples include: Kristin Anderson, Trena Bradley, Leslie Cramer, Thomas Hart, Todd Mullin, Mary Ann Pineo, Julia Smith, Vanessa Staudacher, Anna Lisa Storey, and Pam Vazquez. Along with their help, I have been supported by generous colleagues at IntelliTools, especially Paula Weinberger. Arjan Khalsa, Carol Stanger, Cyndy Hoberman, and Suzanne Feit. Dave Edyburn and the gifted contributors to his journal, *Special Education Technology Practice,* have supplied me with countless resources and ideas. Amy Dell at The College of New Jersey and their journal, TECH-NJ, have provided numerous case studies. Joy Zabala is a generous and thoughtful leader in the field, whose advice I value.

My colleagues and friends at SJSU, Karen Reynolds, Robertta Barba, Elba Maldonado-Colón, and Susan Meyers have made it possible to get help and encouragement when I needed it. Robert James helped with permissions, proofing, and indexing. I will be forever grateful to Karl Murray and Gil Guerin, lifetime mentors, who have always provided the extra support and nudges I needed to move on a new project. At Allyn & Bacon, I've appreciated the assistance and guidance of Virginia Lanigan and Erin Liedel. Myrna Breskin has been patient and helpful in moving the book through production.

I am especially grateful to my family and friends for their patience and unflagging enthusiasm for my work. My youngest son, Jonathan, 14, has used a computer since he could sit up; he is a fearless and discriminating tester of software, hardware, and lessons;

he has helped me maintain a healthy perspective on what is important in life. Older sons Cameron, who's helped me teach technology to teachers from time to time, and Aaron, who helped design the index, are significant supporters. My husband, David Brick, provides "Technology 911" with skill, patience, and humor, and he has given me more joy and happiness than I imagined possible.

In addition, the following reviewers made helpful suggestions: Dave L. Edyburn, University of Wisconsin, Milwaukee and Joe Nolan, Southwestern Oklahoma State University.

TECHNOLOGY FOR INCLUSION

CHAPTER ONE

A PHILOSOPHY OF EMPOWERMENT

Teaching and Learning with Technology for Students with Disabilities, Their Families, Their Teachers, and Service Providers

"Any sufficiently advanced technology is indistinguishable from magic," noted Arthur C. Clarke, noted science fiction author whose masterwork, *2001: A Space Odyssey,* once again captures our imagination, as we compare our own reality to the imaginary world he created and look back on the technological advances of the past 30 years. "Magic" is a primitive way of describing the sense of empowerment that results from being able to do something you had believed was impossible. Interviews with special educators, students with disabilities, and family members confirm the benefits and breakthroughs that technology can provide, offering students a different way of looking at themselves and their capabilities and providing teachers with a new set of tools to support growth and learning (Lewis, 2000).

As McKenzie notes (2000), "we must move past the current preoccupation with wires, networks and computers. We must move beyond technology for the sake of technology's sake. Information technology does not transform schools by itself" (p. v). He goes on to suggest that "questions and questioning may be the most powerful technologies of all" (p. 1). As you read this book, you might note the questions that come to your mind, rather than looking for answers or information. Each chapter is designed to challenge your thinking about the role of technology as currently seen in most schools, to focus instead on how it *could* be, and to ask the questions that will get us there. For example, what do we know about the impact of technology on the lives and learning of students with disabilities and those who care about them? What barriers remain to our efforts to provide meaningful access to these tools in inclusive environments? What promise does technology hold for these students and their future? These are some of the questions examined in this book, based on reflections by researchers, teachers, therapists, students, and parents, and their day-to-day experiences.

Each revision of this book has brought opportunities to reflect on both the magnitude of change in the field of special education and technology and on the stability of the most powerful ideas. Students and their parents continue to press for access to technology that can expand opportunities for expression, communication, academic success, social participation and inclusion, and preparation for an independent life. Educators and service providers are energized by the experiences of their students and clients with technology and frustrated more than ever by funding shortages and bureaucratic barriers that delay meeting needs. At the same time, many schools are saddled with equipment that is poorly utilized, out-of-date, or inoperative. Schools struggle to retain well-trained teachers and staff who have creative and innovative ways of using technology to get the best from students and to free students to express themselves, engage with real-life learning, and to think independently.

Ideas and examples for this book came from thousands of hours of talking to students, parents, teachers, administrators, service providers, software and hardware designers, and professors who prepare special education personnel. Classroom observations, reviews of research, and pilot tests of lessons, software, and hardware with a wide range of students provide first hand knowledge of what works, what doesn't, and why. As you explore the book, continue to look for questions that can help you find solutions that will work for your students—high-tech, low-tech, no-tech—a balance that fits your situation.

GOALS OF THIS BOOK

By the time you finish this book, you will have:

1. assessed your technology skills;
2. reflected on the current impact of technology in empowering your students/clients/children;
3. developed your skill in using productivity tools and considered their use with your students;
4. reconceptualized inclusion through use of universal design principles to create access to the general education curriculum for all students;
5. reviewed technology applications throughout the curriculum and the life cycle;
6. developed a variety of ways of using the Internet to expand your and your students' horizons;
7. assessed your school's alignment with legislation and policy regarding assistive technology and the IEP;
8. created a vision of what technology offers you and your students.

HOW TO USE THIS BOOK

The sequence of the book is designed to make sure that no aspect of technology implementation is overlooked; however, experienced computer users will feel comfortable skipping around in this book. Because of their origins in actual teacher practice, the examples, worksheets, resource lists, and Web sites are likely to stimulate additional ideas for implementing technology programs.

The first section of the book focuses on empowerment, access, and productivity.

- Chapter 1 introduces the concept of empowerment and technology.
- Chapter 2 focuses on productivity tools of database, spreadsheet, and presentation software, and how teachers, families, and students can benefit from skills with these tools.
- Chapter 3, the concept of "universal design" provides a means of evaluating access to both technology and curriculum, so that students can gain the greatest benefits from technology tools.
- Chapter 4 gives ways of using technology to promote social skills and friendship.

In the second section of the book, the role of technology is examined from several different perspectives.

- In Chapter 5, ways to integrate technology across the curriculum areas of reading, writing, math, social studies, and science are presented, with examples and activities;
- Chapter 6 examines the use of technology designed specifically to augment abilities, bypass disabilities, or compensate for disabilities, as each disability area is considered with specially designed technology;
- in Chapter 7, we look at the role of technology through the life cycle, as young children move into school, children move into adolescence, then on into vocational options. What can technology offer in academic, recreational, social, and life skills areas?

The third section of the book, Chapters 8 and 9, highlights the growing emphasis on the Internet as a tool for learning, communicating, exploring, and providing an audience for one's ideas and interests. Chapter 10 provides a glimpse into the rapidly developing field of virtual reality and its implications for students with special needs.

The last section of the book looks at school- and communitywide issues of technology integration. Chapter 11 provides the legislative mandates and policy that assure access to technology and the collaborative process that makes technology a reality for all students. Chapter 12 offers a variety of choices that schools must make to provide access to technology within the school and to the community. Chapter 13 encourages teachers and students to use technology as a way of building inclusion opportunities within the school and the community through service-learning. Finally, having reflected on all the possibilities that technology has to offer, Chapter 14 asks readers to develop their own vision of technology for empowerment as it fits best in their family, school, and community.

STUDENT ACTIVITIES

1. Look through this book's table of contents and list five questions you have about technology and inclusion that you would like to explore as you read this book. Note the chapters in which you are the most skilled or knowledgeable.

2. Think about your own experience of empowerment (and disempowerment) in using technology. When you were feeling empowered, what were the feelings, thoughts, and fantasies that went through your mind? Briefly summarize what you were able to do with technology

that you previously considered difficult or impossible. When you felt disempowered, what feelings, thoughts, and fantasies went through your mind? What strategies did you use to overcome the disempowerment? Were you eventually successful?

3. Think about the students in your school or community. On a piece of paper, make two columns. Label the first column "Strengths," and list the ways you think your school or community is doing an effective job of providing meaningful access to technology for all students, including those with disabilities. Under the second column, labeled "Ideas for Improvements," note ideas for ways to improve access and use of technology as you read the book.

Strengths	Ideas for Improvement

REFERENCES

Lewis, R. (2000). Musings on technology and learning disabilities on the occasion of the new millennium. *Journal of Special Education Technology, 15*(2), 5–12.

McKenzie, J. (2000). *Beyond technology: Questioning, research, and the information literate school.* Bellingham, WA: FNO Press.

CHAPTER TWO

EMPOWERING TEACHERS, STUDENTS, AND FAMILIES WITH PRODUCTIVITY TOOLS

Teachers, students, and parents alike dream of ways that the tasks they consider "drudgery" could be reduced (or eliminated), saving time for more engaging and stimulating endeavors. Many people who might ordinarily avoid using a computer become dedicated technology users when they see their effectiveness or efficiency enhanced through using software "productivity tools." In this chapter, we will focus exclusively on three types of productivity tools: multimedia presentation software, spreadsheets, and database management. Word processing will be addressed in Chapter 5.

You might be wondering, "What is so special about productivity tools for students with disabilities and their families? Their teachers?" Certainly, productivity tools can be helpful or desirable to any busy person; however, for a child with disabilities and his or her family, time is more precious and more limited; technology may be the only way an idea or need can be expressed. For a special educator, the pressure of time is more intense, and data collection and reporting procedures more demanding.

Because the focus of this book is to assist teachers, students, and families in benefiting from inclusive educational environments through technology, productivity tools for empowerment is an ideal place to begin. In this chapter, you will have a chance to explore:

- multimedia presentation software, which adds a multisensory dimension to anything a teacher or student might ordinarily present verbally (presentations with graphics, sound and music, animation, movies);
- spreadsheets, the next giant step beyond calculators, offer ways in which teachers and students can use their conceptual knowledge to instruct the computer to do repetitive calculations; averaging grades, budgets, and illustrating relationships between numbers using graphs and charts are all done with greater ease and clarity using spreadsheets;
- Database management tools, to organize, sort, and present information in digestible bites; for teachers, databases can be used to store goals and objectives for Individualized Education Programs (IEPs) and student information for reports; for students,

databases help to organize information into categories and to help learners see the connections between "similarities and differences" or "comparisons and contrasts," the staple of essay exams and writing assignments.

CHAPTER GOALS

When you complete this chapter, you will be able to:

1. design a slide show to present instructional content/concepts to your students; teach your students to design their own slide shows;
2. assess the benefits and the limitations of presentation software;
3. create spreadsheets and charts for gradebooks, budgets, and collect data for action research projects;
4. teach your students to use spreadsheets to manipulate numbers and to present data graphically;
5. design a database to organize information such as IEP goals/objectives, student information, and curriculum concepts;
6. teach your students to use databases to organize information for reports.

WHAT IS MULTIMEDIA PRESENTATION SOFTWARE?

"Understanding multimedia as a tool for learning requires more than simply knowing about the latest technical developments. Multimedia introduces into a classroom whole new ways of thinking about curriculum, interactions with students, even the nature of learning itself" (Mageau, 1994). The power of multimedia and hypermedia presentation software comes with changes in the ways teachers and learners have access to and demonstrate their understanding of knowledge, moving from a single dominant presentation and demonstration style (verbal/linguistic, linear/sequential) to an integrated, multisensory learning and demonstration "microworld" (Papert, 1992), where learners have more freedom of choice in the mode of learning and the order in which learning takes place.

Presentations incorporate text, sound, pictures, graphics, animation, video, and links to Web sites, and can include narration (done by the teacher or students). Visual images, digital or scanned photos, can be collected from the Internet. They also can include existing material from word processing, spreadsheet, or graphics programs.

Teachers who have used presentation software with their students on projects such as state or country reports, issues such as alcohol, AIDS, and environmental concerns, report high motivation and use of talents that often are not emphasized in school (Collins, Hawkins, & Carver, 1991). Benefits reported by teachers include: (1) classmates' interest in their peers' presentations; (2) high level of attention and detail; and (3) no apparent differences in quality between students in general or special education.

FIGURE 2.1   Slide View from PowerPoint: Student State Report

Presentation software such as Microsoft PowerPoint™ or Aldus Persuasion™ offers the user four different views while the slide show is developed: slide view, outline view, slide sorter (or storyboard) view, and notes view. An example of each of these views from a student project is presented in Figures 2.1 through 2.4.

Figures 2.4 through 2.6 present a series of lesson plans that were used to help students in an alternative school develop a PowerPoint "Me-Book" about themselves. These lesson plans could be used to help teachers, students, or families develop a slide show in "mind-sized" bites of about one hour each.

WHAT IS A SPREADSHEET?

A spreadsheet is a table of information organized into rows and columns (see Figure 2.7 for an illustration). The spreadsheet does for arithmetic and math problems what the word processor does for written language. Spreadsheets can do calculations when appropriate formulas are entered, and, when a change is entered in one cell or entry, all other entries affected by the change are automatically made. Some examples of commonly available spreadsheets are Microsoft Excel™ (part of the Microsoft Office suite of productivity tools, which include PowerPoint, Excel, and Word) or ClarisWorks™. The Cruncher is a spreadsheet program designed specifically for use in classrooms. It teaches students how to use spreadsheets and graphs in everyday life. It computes, graphs, and talks, and enables students to add animated illustrations and sound effects to their work. The program comes

My State Report is New York

By Thomas

Mr. Larson's 5th grade

Facts

o New York state fish is the native brook trout. The capital is Albany. The state tree is the sugar maple and the state fruit is an apple. The state muffin is an apple muffin.

History

o Giovanni da Verrazano was the first European to sail to New York. He did it in 1524. New York City used to be called New Amsterdam. In 1788, New York

o Became the eleventh state. In 1971, there was a lot of fights in a jail called the Attica State Correctional Facility. Forty-three people died in the fights.

Land Features

o New York is by the Atlantic Ocean. The highest point is Mount Marcy. There are 18 million people that live in New York City. The Statue of Liberty is in the ocean next to New York.

Animals

o There are many animals in New York. Black bears, white tailed deer, red foxes, opossums, skunks, grey squirrels, woodchucks and raccoons.

New York

o I like the state New York because it is a neat place because the pictures in the books about New York are beautiful. There are tall skyscrapers and lots of taxis in the pictures. I like milk and there are lots of dairies in New York. This is my report.

FIGURE 2.2   Outline View from PowerPoint: Student State Report

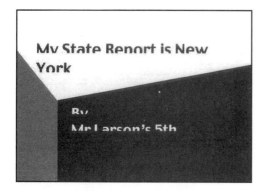

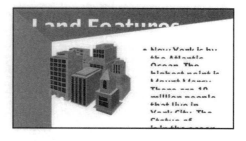

FIGURE 2.3   Slide Sorter View from PowerPoint: Student State Report

Today's Work Plan — Lesson 1

1. Pull down File menu. Select "New."
2. Click on "Presentation Designs." Select the design you want (scroll through options).
3. Click on the layout you prefer for your title slide.
4. Type in the title:
5. Pull down the "Insert" menu and click on "new slide."
6. Click on the layout you want for the new slide. Consider adding clipart? A digitized photo? Sound? Music? Animation?
7. Double click on clip art icon, scroll through list, select something that illustrates some part of your personality, hobbies, or attributes. Or save a space for a digitized photo. Will you want sound or music? What sort of transition will you want to the next slide?
Will you want animation?
8. Save your powerpoint presentation.

Me-book	In Progress	Complete
Storyboard outline-what themes will my book contain?		
Title slide		
Opening slide		

FIGURE 2.4

Today's Work Plan — Lesson 2

1. Start PowerPoint and find your slideshow.
2. Pull Down Insert menu and select Movies and Sound. Select "Sound from Gallery."
3. Click on a sound you like. Click "Insert."
4. Pull down View and select SlideShow. Try out your sound effect.
5. Pull down View and select Slide. Click on a text box.
6. Pull down SlideShow and select "Preset Animation."
7. Select some animation for your text.
8. Pull down View and select SlideShow. Try out your animation.
9. Use "transition" to make the changes from slide to slide more interesting. Pull down Slideshow menu and select "Slide Transition." Scroll through the list of possible transition effects and choose one to try, or choose "random" and let the computer choose it for you!
10. Try out the different views of your slideshow: Slide, outline, storyboard, and slideshow.

11. <u>Save</u> your file in the Folder to share with the class.

Me-book	In Progress	Complete
Three slides – first draft		
Art		
Sound effect		
Animation		
Transition		
Editing for quality: Creativity, accessibility, authenticity, artistic/design (Can you show your work <u>with pride</u> to your friends? Your teachers? Your family?)		

FIGURE 2.5

Today's Work Plan - Lesson 3

1. Start PowerPoint and find your slideshow.
2. Pull Down Insert menu and select "new slide."
3. Click on the blank layout.
4. Pull down Insert and select "Text".
5. From the menu across the bottom, select WordArt (looks like a capital A sort of on its side).
6. Select the word art design you like.
7. Enter some text.
8. Pull down Autoshapes. Select the Lines menu, and choose the squiggly line at the very end. Add some freehand art to one of your slides.
9. Try out the different views of your slideshow: Slide, outline, storyboard, and slideshow.
10. <u>Save</u> your file in the Folder to share with the class.
11. Edit your slideshow. Your slide show should now have:
    • a storyboard with identified themes and a sequence that makes sense
    • scanned photos
    • text describing the photos
    • animation
    • transitions
    • sound effects
    • your own recorded voice
    • word art text
    • freehand drawing

Me-book	In Progress	Complete
Five slides – first draft		
Word Art		
Freehand drawing		
Editing for quality: Creativity, accessibility, authenticity, artistic/design (Can you show your work <u>with pride</u> to your friends? Your teachers? Your family?)		

FIGURE 2.6

FIGURE 2.7   Example of a Spreadsheet

Last Name	First Name	Test 1	Test 2	Test 3	Ass't 1	Ass't 2	Ass't 3	Total Pts	Asst	Test Average	Total
Frost	Sam	89	98	88	20	25	22		67	91.6666667	158.666667
Harris	Claire	56	75	78	22	19	21		62	69.6666667	131.666667
Landry	Fran	87	88	90	25	23	20		68	88.3333333	156.333333
Mallick	Bill	65	60	70	21	24	0		45	65	110
Newsome	Stan	57	65	77	20	25	15		60	66.3333333	126.333333
											0
Average		70.8	77.2	80.6	21.6	23.2	15.6		60.4	76.2	136.6

The Cruncher is a trademark of Vivendi Universal Interactive Publishing North America, Inc., and its subsidiaries and is used with permission.

FIGURE 2.8   Cruncher Lesson Plan: Which Popcorn Should I Buy?

Is it worth it to buy those fancy gourmet brands of popcorn (you know—the ones that promise "to pop up twice as big as regular brands")? You can test different brands and see for yourself.

Buy several different brands of popcorn at the grocery store. Be sure you record the price of each package you buy; enter that number in row 5. Measure the number of cups of popcorn in the entire package; enter that number in row 6. Your class could divide into groups and each group test a different brand of popcorn.

Carefully measure the unpopped kernels, enter that number in row 8, put the kernels into the popcorn maker, and turn it on! Before you let anyone dive into the popcorn, carefully measure the popped popcorn and enter that value in row 9.

Use **Fill Right** in rows 7, 10, and 11. The calculations will be done for you!

Compare the cost per cup of popped corn for different brands. Is that the only criterion you will use in choosing a brand of popcorn?

Would it make more sense to weigh the popped popcorn instead of measuring its volume?

(continued)

FIGURE 2.8   Continued

Brand of popcorn tested	Crazy Pops	Farmer Bill's Corn
Cost of bag of popcorn (unpopped)	$3.19	
Cups in bag of popcorn (unpopped)	3.75	
Cost/cup (unpopped)	$0.85	
Cups unpopped popcorn tested	0.5	
Cups popped popcorn made	13.75	
Expansion factor	27.5	
Cost/cup (popped)	$0.03	

The Cruncher is a trademark of Vivendi Universal Interactive Publishing North America, Inc., and its subsidiaries and is used with permission.

with ten real-world projects with templates to get started. An example of a spreadsheet lesson is included in Figure 2.8.

Regardless of the specific spreadsheet program used, the terminology and the principles are basically the same. A *cell* is the intersection of a row and column, identified by coordinates such as A1, B2, and so on. Each cell holds one piece of information that can be either a *label* (word), a *value* (number), or a *formula* (directions to perform a calculation such as addition, subtraction, multiplication, division, or averaging of values in one or more cells). The *workspace* is the area at the top of the spreadsheet where values, labels, and formulas are entered. The portion of the spreadsheet that can be seen at one time is called a *window*.

PRESENTING SPREADSHEET DATA IN CHARTS AND GRAPHS

The charting feature of spreadsheet programs makes it easy for students and teachers alike to take numbers and data and transform them into charts or graphs, making it easier to display what the numbers mean. Figure 2.9 provides an example of data from a spreadsheet also presented in a bar chart.

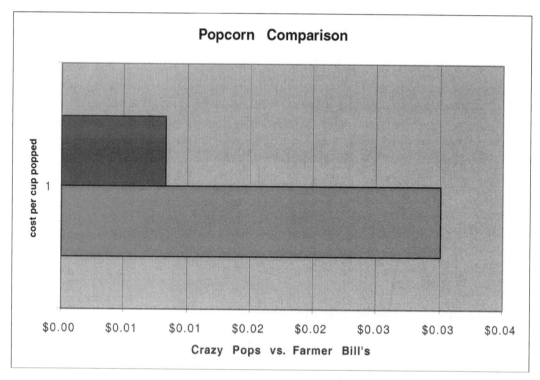

FIGURE 2.9 Bar chart from spreadsheet data

WHAT IS A DATABASE?

In the Information Age classroom, all students need to know how to organize and present information in a variety of ways. Many students (and many adults) struggle with strategies to sort, categorize, and represent information from a variety of sources. Using database tools, students and teachers can become more productive and feel more powerful in dealing with an expanding knowledge base (Roblyer & Edwards, 2000)!

A database is a set of categorized pieces of information or data that can be electronically compared or sorted. For example, a "Classroom" database (shown in Table 2.1 on page 18), would contain a "record" about each student. Each record is made up of "fields," items of information about the student, address or birth date, for example. With a classroom database (or student information file), a teacher can easily access the information needed for a variety of tasks (which students' triennial reviews are coming up? Whose birthdays are coming up?)

Perhaps the biggest challenge in transforming teaching from the transmission of facts for rote memory is helping students analyze information, sort it, and represent it in meaningful ways. Many teachers, who could not survive without the word processor, find the value of database tools more difficult to grasp. Other teachers with "information overload," who have seen the benefits of databases, find the database essential. "A database is one of the computer tools that students should be able to use by the end of elementary school" (Heine, 1994).

At the elementary level, virtually every teacher requires a state or country report, with categories of information that students research using encyclopedias, on the Internet, and with atlases. Some teachers help students use commercially prepared databases to find the information they need; relatively few teachers take this learning opportunity to a more sophisticated level by teaching students to make a classroom database of the information they collect: thinking critically about what information is important, how the computer could help with making comparisons, and how the information might be represented.

Examples of such lessons databases are included in Figures 2.10 through 2.12.

FIGURE 2.10   State or Country Report

Grade Level: 4–12

Content Area: Language, Social Studies, Social Skills, Critical Thinking

Goal: Students will create their own databases, enter the data, sort the data, and print the information.

Time Required: 3–5 hours

Preparation: Materials needed for each student: paper and pencil; menu of ideas (teacher- or student-generated); reference card to use the database program.

Conducting the Lesson:

1. Introduce the assignment; review the steps in designing a database.
2. Review the instructions for using the database program.
3. Discuss the "fields" of information appropriate for a state or country report (e.g., population, capital city, geographic features, products exported, types of industry).
4. Students who have selected the same state or country may work together. Have students complete a paper "form" and complete the fields the class selects by doing research in almanacs, encyclopedias, and on the Internet.
5. When the form is completed, the student(s) enter the information into the class state or country database, so that similarities and differences among states and countries can be compared using the sorting/filtering features of the data base.
6. The completed database is printed for each student to use in preparing their individual report or presentation.

FIGURE 2.11   Class Surveys

Adapted from Judd-Wall (1996)

Grade Level: All

Content Area: Math, Social Studies, Social Skills

Goal: Students will create their own databases, enter the data, sort the data, and print the information.

Time Required: 1–3 hours

Preparation: The teacher selects a topic for the survey (or helps the students in selecting their own). Possible topics: characteristics of their favorite music, favorite vacation destinations, favorite actor/actress, or favorite movie.

Conducting the lesson:

1. If necessary, the teacher can provide a script for students to use in approaching other students to conduct their survey ("Hello, will you do my survey, please? What characteristics are important to you in your favorite type of music? [List the choices.] Thank you for helping me gather my data.")
2. Select a location and time of day students will do the surveying. Have students rehearse so they feel comfortable gathering the data.
3. When students return to the classroom, have them enter it into the database. Then help them analyze the data they've brought back, beginning with making a prediction about what type of music is most popular.
4. Sort/filter the data (How many sixth graders preferred classical music? How many chose music based on the artist?) and analyze the results using charts or graphs.

FIGURE 2.12   Fields for a State or Country Report Data Base

Name of Country or State: _____

Population: _____

Capital City: _____

Geographic Features: _____

Types of Industry: _____

Products Exported: _____

Significant Native Flora: _____

Significant Native Fauna: _____

Significant Historical Events: _____

CURRICULUM INTEGRATION

Now let's take the main ideas introduced in this chapter and tie them together. In the first section, you learned how to teach students to design a slide show with information about themselves. Then you learned how to prepare a spreadsheet that summarized a survey about student characteristics and interests and present it in chart form. Finally, you learned how to design a database so that student information could be retrieved, sorted, and compared, using a "filter" or criterion (e.g., how many students are Eminem fans?) Each productivity tool adds a unique, empowering aspect to the same collection of facts or information.

As you proceed through the book, think about how all the concepts, ideas, tools, and activities can be integrated to work synergistically in improving student and teacher productivity and empowerment.

Perhaps the greatest tool for enhancing personal productivity for teachers is the integrated database/word-processing function, offered by such programs as ClarisWorks, AppleWorks, and Filemaker Pro. By designing a database thoughtfully and with care, and merging it with unlimited forms and form letters created by the word processor, a teacher can perform almost any task related to information about students to communicate with school personnel or parents.

The teacher should consider the information needed about the students and ways in which it is used. He or she should then make a list of all the different types of information that are requested (lists of students with categories of services, such as free lunches, primary language; IEP review dates, birth dates, parents' or guardians' names, addresses, phone numbers, and E-mail addresses). By taking the time to design an effective database and entering the data, the teacher can produce a report for virtually any purpose with just a few keystrokes and no headaches!

For example, Ms. Jones has 31 students in her fourth-grade class: 6 are English-language learners, 4 receive special education services, and 13 receive Chapter I assistance. She thought carefully about the database that could assist with parent conference notices, class lists (which seemed to change daily), meeting dates to review individual plans, and letters home. Because she planned to use form letters, which could merge database information, she chose the fields as listed in the following table.

TABLE 2.1   Classroom Database Fields

Student's last name _____   Student's first name: _____

Title: _____ Father's last name: _____ Father's first name: _____

Title: _____ Mother's last name: _____ Mother's first name: _____

Title: _____ Guardian's last name: _____ Guardian's first name: _____

Father's Work Number: _____   Mother's Work Number: _____

Guardian's Work Number: _____   Student's Date of Birth: _____

Primary Language of the home: _____

Special Education Services (y or n)   Chapter I (y or n)   Free lunch (y or n)

Areas of Strength: _____

Areas of Concern: _____

Once the data for each of her students had been entered, Ms. Jones could print out any lists she needed. She could also send out academic or behavioral progress reports to specific parents, or to all the parents in the class, with personalized information inserted automatically by the computer. Parents who did not speak English would receive a letter in the appropriate language of the home. New fields could be added as needed without having to redo the database or reenter data. Reports could be designed with just the appropriate information needed, such as a list of birthdays for each month for the room mother, or a list of IEP meetings (also using birth dates) for the students in special education. Name and address labels for letters home to families could be done with the same database! Even better, Ms. Jones's template for this year's database can be used again, with next year's students, without starting from scratch.

STUDENT ACTIVITIES

1. Design a PowerPoint presentation to present a lesson to students. Print it out in "handout" format, outline format, and slide format. List three ways that having classroom presentations easily available in different formats could support effective inclusion.

2. Think carefully about the strategies you use to teach mathematics, social studies, and science. Select one aspect of your teaching you would like to expand by using a spreadsheet. Design the spreadsheet. Practice entering data, and creating charts to represent the data.

3. List three ways you could use a database to enhance your own productivity. Design a database that could help you keep track of your students. Practice sorting the data by category and print the lists (e.g., students with IEPs in May).

4. Visit a classroom where a teacher is using a productivity tool (presentation software, spreadsheets, or databases) to assist with instruction. Summarize the strengths of the lesson and describe any challenges the teacher faced in presenting the lesson. What ideas did you get from your observation (things to try or pitfalls to avoid).

REFERENCES

Collins, A., Hawkins, J., & Carver, S. (1991). A cognitive apprenticeship for disadvantaged students. In B. Means, C. Chelemenr, and M. S. Knapp (Eds.), *Teaching advanced skills to at-risk students* (pp. 216–243). San Francisco: Jossey-Bass.

Heine, E. (1994). The world at their fingertips. *The Florida Technology in Education Quarterly, 7*(1), 38–42.

Judd-Wall, J. (1996). Curriculum blending: Computerized surveying activities for everyone. *Learning and Leading with Technology, 23*(8), 61–64.

Mageau, T. (1994). The (in)sane person's guide to multimedia in education. *Electronic Learning, 14*(3), 28–40.

Papert, S. (1992). *The learning machine.* New York: Basic Books.

Roblyer, M., & Edwards, J. (2000). *Integrating educational technology into teaching.* Upper Saddle River, NJ: Prentice-Hall.

CHAPTER THREE

BUILDING THE UNIVERSAL DESIGN CLASSROOM

Academic Curbcuts for All Students

Imagine for a moment a classroom where students were reading a book and writing a report on what they'd read. This seemingly basic learning task poses major challenges for many students, and is a stumbling block to effective inclusion for students with disabilities. Today, however, with digital tools and a fundamental shift of paradigm about learning design, any classroom could offer all learners flexible responses to their learning needs—not just students with disabilities, but every student!

Special educators for a generation have sought tools to encourage general education classroom teachers to accept students with disabilities in their classrooms. "Universal design" principles and tools turn this notion of inclusion upside down. Just as architects have incorporated universal design to create streets with curbcuts and buildings such as the Guggenheim Museum, whose galleries feature sweeping ramps that accommodate the

FIGURE 3.1 Using digital tools, every child can participate in learning activities.

(Photo courtesy of IntelliTools; used with permission.

widest spectrum of users, universal design in classrooms means using digital tools to create alternatives for students with the widest range of abilities, interests, learning styles, and multiple intelligences.

Current research estimates that up to 40 percent of the students in any one classroom would benefit from adjustments of the "standard" curriculum to make learning more efficient and effective. With universal design principles and tools, educators, service providers, and parents can provide a learning environment where all students can succeed.

CHAPTER GOALS

In this chapter, you will explore:

1. what "universal design" means and how it works in a classroom;
2. how universal design addresses current brain research;
3. software that incorporates universal design principles;
4. what you can do to promote universal design in your classroom, school, and community.

UNIVERSAL DESIGN: WHAT IT MEANS AND HOW IT WORKS

The principles of universal design are easiest to understand in the world of architecture and building. Adaptability is subtle, integrated into the design, and benefits everyone. The automatic door and the curbcut are the most concrete and successful examples of universal design principles in action. Our approach to thinking about the way things should be has shifted from asking, "Why should we have to make changes to accommodate a few people in wheelchairs?" to an appreciation of how much better things can be for *all* of us when we pay attention to the needs of everyone.

In the classroom, universal design produces a similar, and equally common sense, revolution in thinking (CAST). Four fundamental shifts in our ideas of teaching and learning occur:

1. students with disabilities fall along a continuum of learner differences, just as other students do;
2. teachers should (and many do) make adjustments for all students, not just those with disabilities;
3. curriculum materials should be as varied and diverse as the learning styles and needs in the classroom, rather than textbook-centered (currently possible with digital and on-line resources);
4. rather than trying to adjust the students to learn from a set curriculum, the curriculum should be flexible to accommodate a range of student differences.

Howard Gardner's research (1985), in which he defines *intelligence* as "an ability to solve problems, or to create products that are valued within one or more cultures," documented seven intelligences (he has since added emotional intelligence to his list, creating eight intelligences).

Gardner and others (Armstrong, 1998; Silver, Strong, & Perini, 2000; Teele, 2000) argue that these multiple intelligences mean that no two students learn exactly the same way; the degree to which pedagogy and curriculum can be flexible and differentiated is the degree to which all students might find success and joy in learning. In this era of increased emphasis on standardized tests as a measure of student achievement, we have moved farther and farther away from what research has documented and what most teachers have known intuitively all along. Some have advocated determining a student's dominant "intelligence" and teaching accordingly, a task that seems logistically daunting to most teachers, and of dubious validity to researchers.

Another approach to the issue of addressing student difference is to use the inherent flexibility that digital tools offer, so that teachers can differentiate instruction without having to categorize or sort students, resort to even more testing, or spend inordinate amounts of preparation time. While teachers may acknowledge that all students learn differently, they have never had the tools to easily make the curriculum flexible and adaptable for those differences until the digital age. Using digital tools to make the curriculum accessible, the teacher can respond to those needs without stigmatizing or blaming students with disabilities for the extra work required. Universal design features of these digital tools provide the framework for the multiple intelligence classroom.

UNIVERSAL DESIGN AND CURRENT BRAIN RESEARCH

Recent research documents the existence of three interconnected and interdependent systems within the brain: recognition systems (identifying patterns), strategic systems (generating patterns), and affective systems (determining priorities through emotions and feelings). The size of the regions devoted to each of these systems is different for each person, which is reflected in different types of learning style, strengths, and weaknesses. For example, in Einstein's brain, the recognition system was strongest in the dimension of spatial cognition; he had severe difficulties in recognizing the letter patterns and learning to read, but he was a genius in discovering the fundamentals of physics. His teachers were limited in what they could do: (1) their beliefs about intelligence were traditional; and (2) digital tools were not available to adapt his learning environment.

Universal design using digital tools provides maximum adaptability in three dimensions:

1. **multiple means of representation,** which provide choices to suit varied recognition systems;
2. **multiple means of expression and control,** with choices for different strategic systems;
3. **multiple means for engagement,** targeted to the affective system, with different ways of holding students' attention and motivating them to learn (Meyer & O'Neill, 2000a).

The figure below (Orkwis & McLane, 1998) illustrates the relationship between the three different aspects of Universal Design for Learning.

MULTIPLE MODES OF REPRESENTATION

Meyer and O'Neill (2000b) describe Martin, a student with difficulties doing the extensive reading required by his science course. He is good at sports, enjoys music, and is very social, but reading is not his best way of getting information.

When his class studies the human body, Martin has difficulty grasping the major organ systems and their interrelationships, primarily because this information is being presented exclusively via a printed textbook.

Martin might be able to understand the human body more easily were he able to use a program such as ADAM, the Inside Story (ADAM Software, Inc.). This CD-ROM program

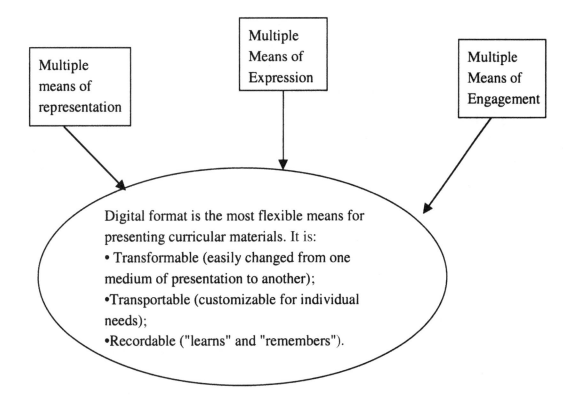

FIGURE 3.2   Essential Qualities of Universal Design (CAST)

presents information in multiple media, including still pictures, animations, speech, and text. Unlike Martin's science textbook, where printed words and illustrations are the only alternatives for conveying critical content, programs like ADAM can use animation to demonstrate relationships, speech to reinforce concepts, and color, sound, and other media to highlight important facts. The essential information is represented in multiple ways.

(What Meyer and O'Neill don't mention is that the same program might help students whose native language is not English, students who read well but slowly, or high achievers who just prefer working on the computer. The use of ADAM doesn't require students to provide a reason or to be stigmatized for their preferences, as is the case in traditional "mainstreaming" or "inclusion" within the general education classroom.)

MULTIPLE MODES OF EXPRESSION

Students in a seventh grade class are studying Spanish. They need to demonstrate their mastery of vocabulary, verb forms, and ability to communicate in the Spanish language. The teacher gives them a range of choices for demonstrating their learning, in addition to worksheets and quizzes. They can use videotape to act out a dialogue or present a skit or play. They can use PowerPoint™ to do a presentation in Spanish on some aspect of the culture in which they are interested. The presentation can include music, art, photos as well as text to capture student interest. Students with difficulty expressing themselves in front of a group can let the computer read their work aloud or they can record their presentation and let the students hear their voices, but in a less stressful mode.

Many researchers have documented the impact of multiple options for expression on achievement (Armstrong, 1998; Silver, Strong, & Perini, 2000; Teele, 2000). Students with certain gifts or skills can use art, photography, drama, music, and video to demonstrate their learning. Students benefit from seeing that they all learn differently, which reduces the pressure to put down or scapegoat a student who is a poor reader or makes low grades on multiple-choice tests.

MULTIPLE MODES OF ENGAGEMENT

The two scenarios just presented also help to illustrate the principle of multiple modes of engagement. Teachers can balance the forces of challenge and support so that students don't become discouraged by low rates of success at the beginning of a learning task or by being compared to other students who may learn differently. Progressive challenges with built-in scaffolds for success ensure that motivation is not stifled.

Students are usually attracted to new and interesting activities, but they also need an appropriate degree of structure, feeling comfort in the familiar. Teachers and students need curriculum materials that can vary the amount of repetition, surprise, familiarity, and randomness.

Thinking about cultural and developmental issues also helps teachers provide motivation and encouragement for learning. Giving students a chance to do activities that resonate with their own background experience makes learning "real" and meaningful.

SOFTWARE WITH UNIVERSAL DESIGN PRINCIPLES

The computer is like a chameleon: it has the capability to offer multiple environments and tools all in one: VCR, calculator, phone, CD player, video game, drafting table, battlefield, chemistry lab. Because of its chameleonlike qualities and its ability to do many things at once, digital tools offer the greatest flexibility for providing Universal Design for Learning. The first software designed explicitly with Universal Design for Learning principles was Wiggleworks™. WiggleWorks™ provides an alternative to a printed reader, in which the students control:

1. whether the book is read aloud or not, at what pace, in what language;
2. access to definitions (read aloud or not) and pronunciations by clicking a button;
3. the size and color of the text;
4. animation and graphics;
5. the pace of the story as it is read;
6. page-turning (for students with physical disabilities);
7. the option to record their own voice as they read the story, with or without computer narration.

Wiggleworks was developed out of the experience of one kindergartener named Matt, who had cerebral palsy and was learning in an inclusive classroom. Because Matt couldn't talk or move any part of his body except his chin and his eyes, the staff of the Center for Applied Special Technology (CAST) designed electronic books for him. When other students saw the way Matt was learning to read and write, they crowded around him. They wanted to learn that way, too! David Rose of CAST noted: "Our work with Matthew taught us a lesson. If you are careful to design products that are good for students with special needs, these products are good for all students" (O'Neill, 2000b). Through a joint effort with Scholastic, Wiggleworks was created, and thousands of students, with and without disabilities, have been learning to read and write with help from a computer.

In the latest edition of Encarta 98 for Windows, Universal Design for Learning is provided by offering audio and video; the additional sensory inputs may make concepts clearer than they would be with text alone. Audio and video are captioned (providing access to students who are deaf or students who may learn best with a combination of representations).

Access to Math (Don Johnston, Inc.) enables teachers to create a worksheet and adjust the program to alert students to any mistakes being made while they are working on a problem; they can correct mistakes as they work. Students get feedback on their work both visually and auditorily; this immediate feedback helps students improve their performance and keep track of their learning.

CAST's eReader™ reads any text aloud and provides multiple options for controlling the size and color of text, highlighting key points, and speed of presentation. Students can use eReader with any digital text, such as works of literature found on the Internet. One student used eReader with works of Hawthorne and Poe he had found on-line, along with its note-taking capability, to increase his reading speed and comprehension (O'Neill, 1999).

Although providing access to text through computer or audiotaped narration is sufficient for some students, for many, additional supports are needed. Deshler and Schumaker (1981) found that students using audiotapes to provide access to information did not improve student performance. However, when the tape includes strategies to help students organize the information and remember it, performance increases considerably. The latest CAST project, Strategic Reader, combines text-to-speech, highlighting, and study supports to help students differentiate key points from details and to organize and remember what they've read (O'Neill, 2000a).

TEACHER AND PARENT ROLES IN PROMOTING UNIVERSAL DESIGN

What are the first steps that teachers and parents can make to ensure that all students have access to classrooms where Universal Design for Learning principles are in place? Many teachers and parents are not aware that current legislation provides support for access to digital tools and that they should be requesting these features whenever they, their school, or school district orders textbooks, videos, or curriculum materials. The Telecommunications Act of 1996, for example, requires that:

1. all texts (textbooks, etc.) be available in digital format;
2. all videos have captions and educationally relevant descriptions;
3. descriptions for images and graphic layouts be provided in audio (Orkwis & McLane, 1998).

Converting core curriculum materials to accessible digital format may seem like an overwhelming task, but the potential outcomes for students are equally awe-inspiring.

A consortium of teachers and parents has been formed to provide a forum for sharing and advocating for making the shift toward Universal Design for Learning (UDL) a reality. Some school districts, such as Concord, New Hampshire, have made a commitment for UDL districtwide. By joining the consortium, the task becomes less daunting as more people become committed and the results are shared.

STUDENT ACTIVITIES

1. In what ways are architectural curbcuts and academic curbcuts (Universal Design Features) similar?

2. Think about a curriculum unit you plan to use. In the following table, list at least one way that you can build Universal Design Features into your unit.

Multiple Modes of Representation (in what ways can students take in information/skill?)	Multiple Modes of Expression (in what ways can they demonstrate their learning and skills?)	Multiple Means of Engagement (in what ways are student interests matched with the type of presentation and type of response?)

3. List three reasons why digital format is so significant to universal design.

4. Visit www.cast.org and describe three ways the site is universally accessible.

5. If you, your classroom, or school has a Web site, submit it for evaluation of accessibility through Bobby at the CAST Web site. Summarize the results.

REFERENCES

Armstrong, T. (1998). *Awakening genius in the classroom.* Alexandria, VA: ASCD.

Deshle, D. & Schumaker, J. (1986). Learning strategies: An instructional alternative for low-achieving adolecents. *Exceptional Children, 52*(6), 583–590.

Gardner, H. (1985). *Frames of mind: The theory of multiple intelligences.* New York: Basic Books.

Follansbee, S., Hughes, R., Pisha, B., & Stahl, S. (1997). Can online communications improve student performance? Results of a controlled study. *ERS Spectrum, 15* (1), 15–26.

Meyer, A., & O'Neill, L. (2000a). Beyond access: Universal Design for Learning. *Exceptional Parent, 30*(3), 59–61.

Meyer, A., & O'Neill, L. (2000b). Tools and materials that support the learning brain. *Exceptional Parent 30*(5), 60–62.

O'Neill, L. (1999). eReader: A technology key for reading success. *Exceptional Parent 29*(11), 34–40.

O'Neill, L. (2000). Computer technology can empower students with learning disabilities. *Exceptional Parent, 30*(7), 72–74.

O'Neill, L. (2000a). Moving toward the vision of the universally designed classroom. *Exceptional Parent, 30* (9), 52–56.

O'Neill, L. (2000b). Seeing past a child's disability: One parent's view of Universal Design for Learning. *Exceptional Parent, 3* (11), 26–32.

Orkwis, R., & McLane, K. (1998). A curriculum every student can use: Design principles for access. ERIC/OSEP Topical Brief. Reston, VA: Council for Exceptional Children.

Rose, D., & Meyer, A. (1996). Expanding the literacy toolbox (Literacy Research Paper 11). New York: Scholastic.

Rose, D., & Meyer, A. (2000). Universal design for individual differences. *Educational Leadership, 58*(3), 39–43.

Rose, D. & Meyer, A. (2000). Universal Design for Learning. *Journal of Special Education Technology, 15*(1), 67–70.

Rose, D., Sethuraman, S. & Meo, G. (2000). Universal Design for Learning. *Journal of Special Education Technology, 15*(2), 56–60.

Silver, H., Strong, R., & Perini, M. (2000). *So each may learn: Integrating learning styles and multiple intelligences.* Alexandria, VA: ASCD.

Teele, S. (2000). *Rainbows of intelligence: Exploring how students learn.* Thousand Oaks, CA: Corwin Press.

CHAPTER FOUR

CREATING CATALYSTS FOR SOCIAL GROWTH:
Cooperative Learning

"What I like about using computers," said one computer "nerd" to his friend as they passed down the bustling college classroom hallway, "is you have all the interactions of a relationship but none of the problems!" This brief vignette illustrates the mind-set that has historically separated the group of educators who are passionate about social development through human interaction, carefully structured to promote acceptance of diversity, and educators who are passionate about the capacity of technology to enhance learning and productivity. A small, but growing, group of educators has chosen to investigate the power of combining these two passions (i.e., promoting social development and utilizing technology) in a synergistic classroom where computers are used as catalysts for human interaction, and lessons using computers are carefully structured to promote communication and sharing with groups of two or three students working together (Parr, 1995; Signer, 1992). In such classrooms, the differences between students with and without disabilities become blurred, and all students become more powerful and productive, both academically and socially.

CHAPTER GOALS

The purpose of this chapter is to equip educators with the skills and confidence to take advantage of two of the most powerful classroom tools: computers and cooperative learning. In this chapter, you will explore:

1. the definition of cooperative learning and how it is different from groupwork at the computer;
2. how to structure lessons using the computer as a tool with principles of cooperative learning;
3. ideas for computer celebrations, clubs, or other events to provide visibility for the achievements of your students with computers;
4. options for social development through computer activities.

PRINCIPLES OF COOPERATIVE LEARNING

Because of the continuing relative scarcity of computers in many classrooms and schools, many teachers have put students in groups at the computer by necessity, but without knowing or using the same principles of cooperative learning that apply to noncomputer lessons. Cooperative learning, however, refers to more than simply placing students in group activities. Cooperative learning is defined as a way of structuring student interaction so that:

- Students know they can be successful only if their group is successful.
- Students are accountable for their individual understanding and mastery of whatever is being taught.
- Students are given specific instruction in the social skills necessary for the group to be successful.
- Students are given the opportunity to discuss how well their group is working and receive feedback to improve future performance (Johnson & Johnson, 1994; Kagan, 1997).

COOPERATIVE LEARNING VERSUS TRADITIONAL GROUPWORK

A summary of the differences between cooperative learning and groupwork is provided in Table 4.1. A clear understanding of these differences will help you understand how to incorporate cooperative learning into your students' computer experiences (Hooper, 1992; Male, Johnson, Johnson, & Anderson, 1986; Polin, 1992).

Cooperative learning groups are based on positive interdependence among group members; goals are structured so that students need to be concerned about the performance of all group members as well as their own. In order for the situation to be cooperative, students must perceive that they are positively interdependent with other members of their

TABLE 4.1 A Comparison of Cooperative Learning and Groupwork

COOPERATIVE LEARNING	GROUPWORK
Positive interdependence	No interdependence
Individual accountability	No individual accountability
Heterogeneous	Homogeneous
Shared leadership	One appointed leader
Shared responsibility for one another	Responsibility for self
Task and group maintenance skills emphasized	Only task emphasized
Social skills directly taught	Social skills assumed
Teacher observes and intervenes	Teacher ignores group functioning
Groups process their effectiveness	No group processing

learning group. This may be achieved by having mutual goals (goal interdependence); by dividing the work task (task interdependence); by dividing materials, resources, or information among group members (resource interdependence); by assigning students differing roles (role interdependence); and by giving joint rewards (reward interdependence).

The students' mastery of the assigned material is assessed to ensure individual accountability. Each student is given feedback on his or her progress, and the group is given feedback on how each member is progressing so that the other group members know whom to assist and encourage. All group members are accountable for mastering the assigned material. In traditional learning groups, individual students are often not held accountable for providing their share of the group's work, and, occasionally, students will "hitchhike" on the work of others.

Cooperative learning groups are typically heterogeneous in ability levels and personal characteristics, whereas traditional learning groups are often homogeneous in membership. All members in cooperative learning groups share responsibility for performing leadership functions in the group, whereas traditional learning groups frequently have a leader assigned to be in charge. In addition to the shared responsibility for leadership, students are held responsible for each other's learning. Students are expected to provide help and encouragement to each other in order to ensure that all members do the assigned work. In traditional learning groups, members are seldom held accountable for each other's learning. The goals of cooperative learning groups focus on bringing each member's learning to the maximum while maintaining good working relationships among members. Traditional learning groups focus primarily on completing the assignment.

Cooperative learning groups present an opportunity for the teacher to observe the groups and give feedback to students on how effectively they are working. Students are also given the time and procedures to process how effectively they are working together. Students need to have a chance to analyze how well their learning groups are functioning and the extent to which they are using their collaborative skills to promote the learning of all group members and to maintain effective working relationships within the group. Students may then plan how to work with each other more effectively the next day and in the future (Johnson, Johnson, & Holubec, 1993). The teacher must teach needed social skills instead of assuming that students will bring these skills to the group.

SYNERGY OF COOPERATIVE LEARNING AND COMPUTERS

Teachers who have introduced cooperative learning into their classrooms see changes in classroom climate as students begin to appreciate each other's strengths and acknowledge each other's individual differences and needs. Teachers also note the powerful influence of social interaction on students' mastery of skills and knowledge. Given appropriate curriculum that emphasizes open-ended tasks with more than one correct answer, students begin talking to each other differently, asking higher-level questions, and seeking out more learning resources (McKenzie, 2000; Sandholtz, Ringstaff, & Dwyer, 1997). Teachers who use cooperative learning have discovered the power of using the human resources (i.e., the students themselves) in the classroom more effectively, which helps avoid the problem of the teacher or the textbooks becoming the source of all knowledge and wisdom and, therefore, the central focus of classroom life.

In classrooms in which computers are integrated effectively with cooperative learning strategies, teachers report an increase in student interest and motivation. Students enjoy showing each other what they are doing with the computer, and they are proud of written work that they have printed. Students huddle together as they master a new computer program or solve a problem, focused intently on the action or situation in the computer environment. Computer time becomes one of the classroom's most valued opportunities or rewards for students.

By carefully structuring a cooperative lesson that uses the computer as a learning tool, many teachers find that student focus, engagement, and productivity are greater than when using either cooperative learning or computers alone. A wonderful synergy unfolds before teachers' eyes (e.g., student teams rotate through a computer learning center; student teams talk to each other and review resource cards with excitement before the teacher uses the computer as a presentation tool to show the next step in a mystery to be solved; small groups of students gather at computer stations in the computer lab, working on cooperatively structured tasks). Regardless of the number of computers or the particular cooperative learning strategy, more teachers are moving toward cooperatively structured computer activities because of the synergistic magic they produce (McKenzie, 2000; Sandholtz, Ringstaff, & Dwyer, 1997)!

When cooperative learning and the computer are combined for instruction, the computer may, depending on the software:

- present the learning task
- provide strategy instructions
- control the flow of activity (e.g., signals when a new task should be initiated)
- monitor learning activities in an objective and efficient manner
- provide reinforcing messages for good performance on all aspects of the task
- keep track of students' responses for future analysis
- tailor learning activities to the students based on pretraining measures and on responses to tasks within the learning sequence
- provide tests on the training materials and, based on students' responses, branches to further strategy instructions
- perform computations to free the cooperative group from lengthy calculations so that members can spend more energy on problem solving and conceptual learning
- provide expert content

Cooperative learning groups allow students to serve as models for one another. Students also assist one another in analyzing and diagnosing the problems being addressed, explaining the material being learned, teaching relevant concepts and procedures to each other, keeping on-task, and sharing their satisfaction and sense of accomplishment.

Two studies compared computer use in cooperative, competitive, and individualistic learning (Johnson, Johnson, & Stanne, 1986a, 1986b). Results of these studies indicate that computers and cooperative learning promoted greater quantity and quality of daily achievement, more successful problem solving, and higher performance on factual recognition, application, and problem-solving test items than did computers and competitive and individualistic learning. Combining competition with computers had an especially negative impact on female students' achievement, achievement motivation, attitudes toward computers, attitudes toward the subject being studied, and confidence in their ability to work with computers. In the technology-rich, cooperatively structured classrooms of the Apple Classroom of Tomorrow longitudinal studies, research confirmed the benefits for students on achievement, initiative, engagement, motivation, self-esteem, and social acceptance (Sandholtz, Ringstaff, & Dwyer, 1997).

ESSENTIAL COMPONENTS OF COOPERATIVE COMPUTER LESSONS

Although there may be differences in the ways in which researchers have identified the essentials of cooperative learning, there seem to be some basic principles that are common among most of the formal cooperative learning strategies being used by teachers. The following description of the essentials is designed to assist you in structuring your own version of cooperative learning.

Assignment to Teams and Team Preparation

The purpose of team assignment is to assure a good heterogeneous mix of students, taking into account gender, race, cultural and language differences, problematic behaviors, and past performance (achievement and communication skills). In the past, schools have made every effort to group students homogeneously by age, ability, and the like, with limited success. Cooperative learning offers teachers an opportunity to capitalize on the benefits of heterogeneous groups. These strategies work particularly well in mainstreaming and inclusive classroom situations.

Some teachers prefer to randomly assign students to teams in order to keep team assignment simple and to demonstrate to students that they are expected to work together in groups, no matter where they are assigned. Assignment to teams can be as simple as having students count off to a certain number or dealing a deck of cards and having students gather in groups of four.

Team preparation activities build a sense of team identity and spirit as well as trust among team members. Teachers may ask students to select a name for their team and display it on a class bulletin board. For example, students may select team names such as Cyberstars, Techtransformers, or Compupros, which link their team identity to the computer. Team activities that are tied to computer use may be conducted as team members are developing working relationships (Anderson, 1989).

Creating Positive Interdependence among Students

Positive interdependence is the feeling among team members that no one is successful unless everyone is successful. The following examples illustrate the types of interdependence and their use with software programs (specific software titles are listed in italics):

- Goal Interdependence: "You're not finished until everyone in the group can explain the pattern for sorting" (Sammy's Science House, Thinkin' Things).
- Task Interdependence: "Each of you will be an expert on a different aspect of the story—one on the setting, one on the characters, one on the plot. You must agree on how to put your story together."
- Resource Interdependence: "I will give only one worksheet to the group. You must record your group's prediction of what the product will look like on the worksheet" (The Factory).
- Role Interdependence: "Each of you will play a crucial role in discovering the solution to the mystery. The jobs are: Taxonomist, Ecologist, Ethnobotanist, and Plant Chemist. Each of you has information the others do not, and you must share your information to solve the mystery successfully" (Rainforest Researchers).
- Reward Interdependence: "Your grade will be made up of the sum of the individual grades on the test."

Most students have had much practice in competitive classroom goal structures (and many have failed in such settings) and some have had experience in individualized special education classrooms; few have had practice in positive interdependence. Therefore, positive interdependence will need to be concretely and clearly communicated, especially when first presented. Otherwise, students may use their usual ways of working to get the job done, and the group will experience problems. For example, before you start your groups, establish why it is important to work in the groups. Make sure students understand the benefits of working together, using statements such as, "You will want to work closely with each other so that your group grade will go up," "You will receive bonus points for your grade for every student who makes 100 percent in the group," and " If your group does all of its work correctly, you can earn the opportunity to be a computer tutor in the kindergarten class."

Individual Accountability

Most teachers who have experienced learning in traditional groups or who have tried using traditional learning groups in their classrooms find that the addition of individual accountability ensures that each student contributes to the group. It helps the teacher in monitoring exactly how much each student has contributed or the level of mastery of each student of the target skills. For example, in a cooperative computer activity each student must be able to explain the activity, produce a printout, or score at a certain level on a quiz. All students must know in advance that they will be responsible individually for demonstrating mastery.

Direct Teaching of Social Skills

Teachers who use cooperative learning successfully place as much importance on the mastery of key social skills as they do on the mastery of the use of the computer for instructional tasks. Most teachers begin with a single social skill, such as praising; they provide examples of praising, solicit examples from students, and frequently list behaviors and words that characterize praising. For cooperative computer lessons, the teacher would review the software to see which social skills are necessary for students to succeed in using the program, and would follow these steps in teaching the targeted skills:

1. label the skill (e.g., "I want you to use the social skill of asking clarifying questions when you read the resource materials for your role in The Great Ocean Rescue")'
2. model the skill (e.g., "I'm going to show you what that looks like and sounds like by playing the role of oceanographer. Listen to my questions and see how they help aid my teammates in helping me to understand the material");
3. practice the skill (e.g., "Now watch this video of a group of students. Write down at least three clarifying questions that you hear. Check with a partner to see if both of you agree");
4. recognize and reinforce the skill when you see or hear it used by the students (e.g., "I heard Shelley in the Computer Cougars group give Greg some praise for his idea to brainstorm possible solutions to the rainforest research problem before they entered a decision on the keyboard").

TABLE 4.2 Social Skills at Various Grade Levels

GRADE LEVEL	TASK-RELATED SOCIAL SKILLS	MAINTENANCE SOCIAL SKILLS
Lower elementary	Check others' understanding	Encourage
	Give ideas	Use names
	Talk about work	Invite others to talk
	Get group back to work	Respond to ideas
	Repeat what has been said	Look at others
	Ask questions	Say "thank you"
	Follow directions	Share feelings
	Stay in seat	Disagree in a friendly way
Upper elementary	Check others' understanding	Encourage
	Contribute ideas	Use names
	Stay on task	Encourage others to talk
	Respond to ideas	Share feelings
	Paraphrase	Use eye contact
	Follow directions	Show appreciation
	Stay in own space	Disagree in a friendly way
Senior high/adult	Check others' understanding	Encourage
	Give information and opinions	Use names
	Stay on task	Acknowledge contributions
	Paraphrase	Use eye contact
	Seek information and opinions	Express appreciation
	Follow directions	Share feelings
	Encourage others to talk	Practice active listening

Source: From *A Guidebook for Cooperative Learning* (p. 57) by D. Dishon and P. Wilson O'Leary, 1984, Learning Publications (P.O. Box 1326, Holmes Beach, FL 33509). Reprinted by permission of Pat Wilson O'Leary.

In addition to providing systematic instruction in these targeted social skills, teachers monitor the groups, using an observation sheet, so that groups receive feedback on how they are improving or increasing use of the target social skill. As an additional incentive, some teachers use bonus points or give a portion of each group's grade based on the group's use of social skills. A sample list of social skills in included in Table 4.2. The list is divided into two categories of social skills: *task*-related social skills (i.e., those skills directly connected to the specific academic task, such as summarizing, recording, and reporting), and *maintenance* social skills (i.e., those skills that are related to helping the team get along with each other, such as praising, encouraging, and making eye contact).

Processing

Processing refers to the portion of the lesson devoted to closure or wrap-up of the activities, during which the teacher provides structured opportunities for students to discuss and process what happened within their group. The best way to ensure that the effectiveness of the groups continues to improve is to provide time for students to share what they contributed to the group, how the group helped each student learn, problems that the group was able to solve, and problems with which the group would like help. In this way, the teacher creates a feeling that everyone is in this together, sink or swim. One way teachers do this is to conduct a "gallery walk" for the entire class to each group's computer, which involves looking at each group's products or results, and asking the group to comment on the strategies they used to work together. Another strategy for teachers is to ask each group to save their work on a floppy, zip disk, or a computer server, and then use the teacher's presentation station (e.g., computer with a projection device or television hookup) to share the results of their work along with reflections about their teamwork. Some teachers use a roving "camera person" to highlight each group's product along with vignettes of the group's work together, which is then shown to the entire class as a two- to three-minute sampler of each group's work processes.

LEARNING TOGETHER WITH COMPUTERS: A COOPERATIVE LEARNING STRATEGY FOR TEACHERS

Imagine that you are planning your first cooperatively structured computer lesson. Once you have selected the objectives and learning outcomes for the lesson, you will want to select a cooperative learning strategy that has the best fit with the objectives of the lesson. Start with an activity with which you're familiar, for example, a successful lesson that you have fine-tuned on numerous occasions. For this particular lesson, you have selected "Learning Together," a cooperative learning strategy that illustrates the use of the essential components of cooperative learning (Johnson et al., 1993). Two sample lessons incorporating the Learning Together strategy are included in Figures 4.1 and 4.2.

The next step is to select the software that matches the outcomes of the lesson (see Step 1 in the sample lesson in Figure 4.1). For example, you might select a word processor

FIGURE 4.1 Learning Together Lesson Plan

Catalina, My Friend

Developed by: Anna Lisa Storey

Grade level: 5th and 6th graders

Subject: English, Creative Writing

Length: Three 40-minute class periods

STEP 1: SELECT A LESSON

Objective/Goal:
In this lesson, students will visit the Web site, Stone Soup Magazine, at *www.stonesoup. com,* read the featured story, *Catalina, My Friend* by Francisca Thomas, and choose one of three writing activities to complete collaboratively.

STEP 2: MAKE DECISIONS

Group Size: Ten groups of 3 students

Group Assignment: Groups will be assigned heterogeneously, but including at least one student in every group who is proficient with the Internet. Students are familiar with working in cooperative groups and the class uses them frequently throughout the day in other curricular areas. The groups have names they have chosen for themselves, and we have spent time as a class working on team-building exercises and team spirit in order to create positive interdependence and respect among all members of the team. Team members rotate every month so that students learn to work cooperatively with many different team members in new situations.

Room Arrangement: The desks are arranged in pods with two teams at a pod, six desks in all. The computers are stationed throughout the room so that each team can work comfortably at them.

Materials Needed: www.stonesoup.com, previously made worksheet with teacher-made questions for the assignment, students' writing journals

Assigning Roles:

Keyboarder: This team member listens attentively to the groups' ideas and contributes his or her own ideas while using the keyboard and the mouse to navigate the Web site. Keyboarder is sensitive to the different rates at which students read the material on the Web site and the team members communicate those needs to the keyboarder.

Summarizer: This team member checks to make sure everyone's ideas have been considered before making a decision and moving on in the assignment.

Checker: This team member makes sure that everything is spelled correctly and correct punctuation was used before moving forward with the assignments.

All three team members are expected to be praisers, giving each other encouragement and positive feedback throughout the assignment.

(continued)

FIGURE 4.1   Continued

STEP 3: SET THE LESSON

Task: The teacher introduces the topic of magazine articles by asking students if they read magazines and which are their favorites. The teacher passes out copies of popular magazines for young people and asks students to spend a few minutes browsing through them and noticing things about the pages, the pictures, and the articles. The teacher then explains that the teams will be exploring a Web site, an online magazine for young people. The students are to log on to *www.stonesoup.com* and follow the links to the featured story by Francisca Thomas, called *Catalina, My Friend.* This story is too long to spend the whole class time reading it, and students are encouraged to spend their free computer time reading the whole story at a later time. For this assignment, students are to read the first three paragraphs of Francisca's story. The third paragraph ends with the sentence "I stared into her deep brown eyes and squeaked again."

Working together, the team is to complete the worksheet of questions, which asks:

Who is the narrator of this story?
How do you know?
What words does Francisca use to let you know?
Why do you think the narrator was in a box?
Using three sentences, what do you think will happen in the next paragraph?

This should complete the first 40-minute class period. In the next period, students will review the paragraph they read during the previous lesson. The students will then work together to choose one of three writing activities to complete. They may choose to write an autobiographical essay in their writing journals about their own earliest memory, write an essay in their writing journal from the point of view of an animal about the animal's earliest memory, or follow the links on the Stone Soup Web site to Projects—The Mailbox—letters, and write an E-mail to Francisca Thomas telling her what they like best about the way she chose to begin her story. They must all choose to do the same assignment. If they choose one of the assignments in which they write in their journals, they must each write their own essay. If they choose to write the E-mail letter, they must each write a draft of the letter in their journals first. Students will send the actual E-mail during the third class period.

During the third class period, the teams will become writing groups in which the students take turns reading the drafts of their essay or their E-mail to each other. Everyone listens politely and thinks about the compliments and suggestions they will offer the writer when he or she is finished reading the work. Once the student is finished reading, team members offer specific compliments and suggestions. Students may use the cue cards they have created for offering such compliments and suggestions that structure the beginning of their statements with openings like: I like the part where…, I want to know more about…, I like the way you described…, Your writing made me feel…. The writers then ask any questions they have for the group about their writing, using their cue cards if they need them to ask questions like: What details should I add? Is there any part that is confusing? What do you want to know more about? Team members answer these questions as the writer asks them. All members have a turn reading their drafts and then students make their revisions based on the suggestions and feedback they received from the team. If the team chose to write the E-mail letters, this is the time for them to type the letter on the computer and send it.

At the end of the period, each team chooses one essay or E-mail from their team for a member to read aloud to the whole class.

FIGURE 4.1 Continued

Type of Positive Interdependence: Group members work together to decide which of the three activities will be most appropriate for all of them.

Individual Accountability: Each group member writes his or her own essay in journals or E-mails to Francisca.

Criterion for Success: A completed essay in their journals or a completed E-mail.

Specific Behaviors Expected: Students are expected to listen to each other and respect each other's ideas and desires. Students are expected to cooperate and come to a consensus if there is a difference of opinion.

STEP 4: MONITOR AND PROCESS

Evidence of Expected Behaviors: The teacher will observe the students reading the first paragraph of the story together, discussing and sharing their ideas with each other, and working on their essays or on their E-mails. The teacher will observe the students working respectfully in their teams on the third day to workshop their writing.

Plans for Processing: At the end of the third class period, students will choose one essay or E-mail from their team to present to the whole class.

STEP 5: EVALUATE OUTCOMES

    Task Achievement
    Group Functioning
    Notes on Individuals
    Suggestions for Next Time

FIGURE 4.2 Lesson Plan for Oregon Trail

Developed by Pam Vazquez

Grade Level: High-school-aged moderate to severely handicapped students

Subject: Social Skills

Length: One hour

STEP 1: SELECT A LESSON

Objective/Goal: The students will work cooperatively together to finish (or play until time runs out) the computer game, *Oregon Trail 3,* by using the roles assigned to them 80 percent of the time.

STEP 2: MAKE DECISIONS

Group Size: Three students and one adult.

Group Assignment: Group assignment will be as heterogeneous as possible. Members will be assigned according to abilities.

(continued)

FIGURE 4.2   Continued

Room Arrangement: One chair will be placed directly in front of the computer. Chairs will be placed on either side of that chair. A chair will be placed in a second row so fiat person can look between the shoulders of the person in the center chair and the shoulders of the person in one of the side chairs.

Materials Needed: Software titled *Oregon Trail 3,* calculator, and activity sheet.

Assigning Roles: Student roles will be Reader, Keyboarder-who listens to group ideas and responds to suggestions as he or she used the keyboard, and Recorder whose job is to fill out the activity sheet and use the calculator as needed. Decision-making is to be shared by the whole group. The adult role will be as a Mediator and Advisor.

STEP 3: SET THE LESSON

Task: The teacher introduces the topic of teamwork. The teacher and students brainstorm instances when they have worked together as a team and when others work together as a team. Together, they will discuss the advantages of working as a team and different ways that teams can work together. The teacher tells the students that today, they will work together as a team in a new way. Students will work together to play the game, "Oregon Trail 3" by using their assigned roles and completing the activity sheets as a group. (The task is to get your wagon party to Oregon alive!)

Type of Positive Interdependence: When students complete the game, or play until time is up, successfully by using the assigned roles and correctly completing the activity sheet, students will be able to put marbles in a jar to earn a pizza party (Made It and Almost Made It). If the team of students reach the end of the trail, they will each earn a foil covered chocolate coin as well (Made It). Each group member contributes ideas and helps the group make decisions. The adult will confirm if the task has been accomplished.

Individual Accountability: The adult Mediator/Advisor will record and redirect any infractions of "role wandering" that seem inappropriate and encourage students to participate and play their role. The adult Mediator/Advisor will record attempts each student made to contribute an idea by a check next to their name.

Criteria for Success:

Made It!
Students will know they have "made it" or have been fully successful during this lesson if they work cooperatively by using the assigned roles 80% of the time, complete the game by arriving in Oregon, and complete the activity sheet with 100% accuracy, given advice from the Mediator/Advisor.

Working Cooperatively	Successful _____	
Using Roles	Successful _____	
Made it!	Roles used 80+% of the time	10 correct
Almost made it	Roles used 75%	7–9
No, time up		
Half-way there	Roles used 70%	64 correct
No, time up		
Barely started		

FIGURE 4.2   Continued

Specific Behaviors Expected: Students will respect the roles that each student plays. Students will show this respect by using the social skills task and maintenance skills for lower elementary. Students will contribute ideas, listen to others' ideas, and help the group come to consensus. Students will do the work corresponding to their tasks. Students will keep hands and feet to themselves.

STEP 4: MONITOR AND PROCESS
Evidence of Expected Behaviors: Finished game or played together until time was up, a tangible product (activity sheet), and recorded observations of Mediator/Advisor.

Plans for Processing: Questions will be asked orally, since many M/S handicapped students are not literate. The teacher will go over the Criteria for Success using paraphrasing in a question and answer approach to draw out answers. A review and discussion of the social skills demonstrated by the group will follow the lesson.

STEP 5: EVALUATE OUTCOMES (Reflect on your lesson when it's over):

OREGON TRAIL ACTIVITY SHEET

Names and Jobs of Group Members:

Keyboarder: _____

Recorder: _____

Reader: _____

Mediator/Advisor: _____

1. Circle the person you are going to be.

   Banker   Carpenter   Farmer

2. What month did you leave in?

   _____

3. Whose general store will you use to buy your supplies?

   _____

4. **Matt recommends 3 yoke of oxen. He charges $40.00 for a yoke. How much will three yoke of oxen cost you?** (Set up the problem. Show your work here.)

5. **You should take 200 pounds of food for each person in your family. You have five people in your family. How many pounds of food will you need to buy?** (Set up the problem. Show your work here.)

(continued)

FIGURE 4.2   Continued

6. **Matt recommends that you buy 2 sets of clothing per person. There are 5 people in your party. How many sets of clothing do you need to buy?** (Set up the problem. Show your work here.)

7. **At the Snake River, you talk to some people. How do they recommend you cross the river that is 1,000 ft across and 6 ft deep?**

with built-in graphics for students to write and illustrate a story, using a read-aloud book as a model (Broad, 1991). You want to be sure that:

■ at least one student in each group can operate the selected software program. You can assign students to groups based on computer experience or skill; you can also use the activity as an opportunity to perform a status treatment (Cohen & Lotan, 1998) with a low-status student (i.e., a low-achieving student, a student included in the classroom from special education, an English-language learner, or a student whose behavior interferes with positive peer relationships). In a *status treatment,* you use a high-status skill (e.g., computer expertise) and assign competence to the low-status student by ensuring that the student has a special ability that can be pointed out to the group (e.g., "Stephen has had a chance to really learn how to use

FIGURE 4.3   A teacher monitors a cooperative group at the computer in a "Learning Together" lesson. (Used by permission.)

this program skillfully; you will want to be sure to get his help as you are learning to use the software"). If necessary, you can pretrain the student in the computer skill in order to make sure that the recognition is authentic.

- Step 2 includes all of the decisions you must make about assigning students to teams, the size of the teams, the materials needed, and the roles you will use with the groups (Anderson, 1995).
- In Step 3, you plan how you will introduce the lesson. You've chosen *Quick as a Cricket* (Wood, 1989) to read aloud to the students, and you've stimulated their curiosity about the book by having them brainstorm their group's names of animals and describing words (i.e., adjectives), which they can then use when they write their own team version of *Quick as a Cricket* on the computer. You set the stage for the cooperative aspect of the lesson by telling the students that their book will consist of three sentences about each team member (positive interdependence and individual accountability) and that you want them to rotate the roles of keyboarder, praiser, and checker. (If these roles are new to the students, you will want to take the time to systematically team them, as described previously.) Your criteria for success are a completed book and reading the book aloud to the class. You will call on one person at random from each team to do the reading, so all students will need to make sure that the whole team can read all of the words.
- For Step 4, you plan how you will observe the group working both at the computer and at a table as the members plan their book, share their sentences, and complete their assignment at the computer. Design an easy-to-use observation sheet so that you can give precise feedback on teamwork during the processing portion of the lesson.
- Step 5 in the lesson-planning format provides you with a place to reflect on the outcomes of your lesson once you have tried the learning strategy with your students.

SELECTING THE ENVIRONMENT FOR COOPERATIVE COMPUTER LESSONS

Successful cooperative computer lessons occur in a variety of environments: the classroom, with one or a few computers; the school computer lab, with enough computers for every student; in the school library, with a few computer stations hooked up to the Internet. Regardless of the location, teachers can design lessons that will work in the environments they have, or they can work to make the environments they have more flexible for cooperative computer lessons.

Computer Laboratory

In some schools, teachers will want to be sure to work collaboratively with the computer specialist, who can be a great asset in helping to select appropriate software, training "expert" students in the chosen software's operation, and making sure that all of the equipment is running smoothly. For teachers fortunate enough to have this extra support, they will want to share their cooperatively structured lesson plan with the computer specialist and solicit his or her participation in all aspects of the lesson (e.g., observing the groups, contributing precise feedback about performance in the processing portion of the lesson). In some situations, the computer lab may, in fact, have enough computers for every student to work alone. That does not mean that teachers must use the computer lab in that way (although it may certainly be appropriate sometimes). If the computer lab is not set up ideally for a cooperatively structured computer lesson, teachers should explore what adjustments are possible. Sometimes computer labs are based on assumptions about teachers preferring "one child, one computer"; asking questions about the room's layout, space for on- and off-computer activities, and space between computer stations that allow room for individuals or small groups to work might improve the usefulness of the computer lab for many teachers. In some cases, teachers need to be creative in using the computer lab to complete a lesson (i.e., thinking about ways their class can fit into the way the computer lab typically operates without sacrificing the goal of their lesson).

Classroom

In classrooms with only one computer, with or without Internet access, teachers use several options (Dockterman, 1997). The teacher can use the computer to do a presentation or overview of the key information that students will need to do their work in cooperative groups or introduce the computer task that students will work on in another setting. The computer can be used as a discussion generator with software such as Decisions, Decisions, in which students in cooperative groups must come to consensus or use a democratic process to decide how to handle an issue. The software presents a problem, with five possible decisions, no right answers: each one has benefits and limitations. Depending on the decision the students select, the computer randomly selects the variables that will affect the success or failure of the outcome of their decision. The computer can serve as a station where students rotate in their cooperative groups to do their writing, analyze the data from a survey they have done, or participate in a simulation (i.e., Rainforest Researchers).

School Library

With a cooperatively structured research task on the Internet, students can work in small groups at stations in the library to gather the information they need. They can bring the information back to the classroom or to the computer lab, where each person can write his or her report, design his or her presentation, or make graphs or charts necessary to illustrate his or her learning. More information on cooperative and individual projects using the Internet will be found in Chapter 8.

A list of software appropriate for cooperative learning in these environments is included in Table 4.3. Research evidence documents the effectiveness of classroom activities such as those described above. In one study (Mevarech, Stern, & Levita, 1987), students were given an achievement test and then assigned at random to an individualistic setting or a paired learning setting, with each pair being approximately equivalent in scores on an achievement test. After two months, students were asked to complete questionnaires on their attitudes toward classmates, computer learning, and cooperative learning. The results showed that students became more altruistic toward their partners in the cooperative setting and preferred cooperative to individualistic learning. Their achievement was also

TABLE 4.3   Social Development Software and Publishers

SOFTWARE	PUBLISHER
Yukon Trail	Learning Company
Oregon Trail	Sunburst
Maya Quest	Sunburst
Colony Quest	Sunburst
Decisions, Decisions	Tom Snyder Productions
Rainforest Researchers	Tom Snyder Productions
The Great Solar System Rescue	Tom Snyder Productions
Nigel's World	Lawrence Productions
Where in the…is Carmen Sandiego series	Learning Company
Sim City series	Maxis
Dig It: Egyptians	Terrapin

slightly higher than that of the students in the individualistic setting, although not statistically significant.

STUDENT ACTIVITIES

1. Design a cooperative computer lesson using software related to the curriculum goal. Try it out. Write a reflection paper that describes your experience. Include your lesson plan.

2. Obtain a copy of one of the programs listed in Table 4.3 (software publishers typically allow teachers a 45-day preview). Analyze the cooperative aspects built into the program by listing the software features next to each of the essential elements of cooperative learning.

REFERENCES

Anderson, M. (1989). *Fitting in: Partnerships at the computer.* Arlington, VA: Ma-Jo Press.

Anderson, M. (1995). *Using HyperStudio in a resource room.* Presentation at San José State University, San José, CA.

Broad, C. (1991). *The writing team with the writing machine.* Santa Cruz, CA: Educational Apple-cations.

Cohen, E. & Lotan, R. (1995). Producing equal status interaction in the heterogeneous classroom. *American Educational Research Journal, 32,*(1), 99–120.

Dockterman, D. (1997). *Great teaching in the one computer classroom.* Watertown, MA: Tom Snyder Productions.

Hooper, S. (1992). Cooperative learning and computer-based instruction. *Educational Technology, Research and Development, 40*(3), 21–38.

Johnson, D., & Johnson, R. (1994). *Learning together and alone.* Englewood Cliffs, NJ: Prentice-Hall.

Johnson, R., Johnson, D., & Holubec, E. (1993). *Circles of learning.* Edina, MN: Interaction.

Johnson, R., Johnson, D., & Stanne, M. (1986a). Computer-assisted instruction: A comparison of cooperative, competitive, and individualistic goal structures. *American Educational Research Journal, 23*(3), 382–391.

Johnson, R., Johnson, D. & Stanne, M. (1986b). The effects of cooperative, competitive, and individualistic goal structures on computer-assisted instruction. *Journal of Educational Psychology, 77*(6), 668–677.

Kagan, S. (1997). *Cooperative learning resources for teachers.* San Juan Capistrano, CA: Kagan Cooperative Learning.

McKenzie, J. (2000). *Beyond technology: Questioning, research, and the information literate school.* Bellingham, WA: FNO Press.

Male, M., Johnson, R., Johnson, D., & Anderson, M. (1986). Cooperative learning and computers: An activity guide for teachers. Santa Cruz, CA: Educational Apple-cations.

Mevarech, Z., Stern, D., & Levita, I. (1987). To cooperate or not to cooperate in CAI: That is the question. *Journal of Educational Research, 60*(2), 68–72.

Parr, D. (1995). *Increasing social awareness and geographical skills of fourth grade students with technology, on-line communications, and cooperativce activities.* Tallahassee, FL: Nova Southeastern University. (ERIC Document Reproduction Service No. ED 389 270).

Polin, L. (1992). Collegial learning: Life with the boyz. *Writing Notebook, 9*(4), 28–32.

Sandholtz, J., Ringstaff, C., & Dwyer, D. (1997). *Teaching with technology: Creating student-centered classrooms.* New York: Teachers College Press.

Signer, B. (1992). A model of cooperative learning with intergroup competition and findings when applied to an interactive video reading program. *Journal of Research on Computing in Education, 25*(2), 141–158.

Wood, A. (1989). *Quick as a cricket.* Swindan, UK: Child's Play International.

CHAPTER FIVE

TECHNOLOGY ACROSS THE CURRICULUM
Reading, Writing, Math, Science, and Social Studies

With the growing emphasis on inclusion of students with disabilities in general education classroom comes a growing responsibility to provide classrooms with tools that deliver instruction in a variety of modes and enable learners to demonstrate their learning in different ways. Computers offer an infinitely adaptable tool with unrestricted possibilities. If students with disabilities are to be meaningfully included in instruction and accompanying assessment, general and special educators must use technology tools that will facilitate their success, rather than assuming that these students will be successful using traditional instructional approaches. Much has been learned as teachers and parents have experimented with different types of software across subject areas and in different learning settings. In this chapter, you will explore a variety of classroom applications of technology designed to improve academic outcomes for students with and without disabilities.

CHAPTER GOALS

By the end of this chapter, you will have explored:

1. promising practices for teachers and parents who want to integrate technology in basic skills and subject area curriculum in K–12 students;
2. how to select software that will engage, stimulate, and promote accelerated achievement in subject area instruction;
3. ways to organize your classroom so that technology is a natural part of learning and teaching, rather than an isolated event.

READING

Software in the area of reading, from acquisition of decoding skills to the development of strategies for improved reading comprehension, has evolved greatly in the twenty years in which computers have been available for classroom use. Considerable research has documented the importance of phonemic awareness in literacy development, and many students with learning disabilities and dyslexia seem to struggle with making sense of the printed word. How can computers help?

Computers provide a multisensory delivery system in which words can be seen, heard, manipulated, color-coded, and linked with graphic cues, automatically! When reading is integrated with writing, computers can:

- ease the fine-motor difficulties that complicate the writing process by reducing the keystrokes (word prediction);
- increase writing production by reducing the pressure to spell words correctly (spell checking);
- provide avenues for writing by students who have physical disabilities or whose keyboarding skills are limited (speech recognition);
- offer students unlimited opportunities for practice and the repetition necessary to build fluency, with continuous corrective feedback (computer-assisted instruction);
- build comprehension by providing strategic prompts as students are reading/listening to content (e.g., eReader or Ultimate Reader).

Phonemic Awareness

One difficulty in literacy development noted by speech and language clinicians and special educators is auditory temporal processing. Groundbreaking research by Tallal (1995) led to the development of Fast ForWord (Scientific Learning Corporation), a computer-based approach to receptive language and auditory processing remediation. Fast ForWard is designed to extend, slow down, and heighten awareness of the smallest "phonetic elements" that make up phonemes. Over an intensive training process, students learn how to "hear" these small speech sounds, which has a dramatic effect on their ability to move through skills taken for granted by many: constructing rhyming words, segmenting words into syllables, and recognizing sound–symbol relationships. "Most children in the studies to date have experienced significant and measurable improvements in acoustic reception, speech reception, and language comprehension abilities. The children have moved from below-average ranges into normal ranges for skills and abilities that are required for normal language use (Earle, 1998, p. 1).

IntelliTools has developed a structured reading instruction program to be used with IntelliKeys and IntelliTalk, which was researched at six sites nationwide with 55 first graders at risk for reading failure or already diagnosed with disabilities. "The students in this study, coming from different geographic regions throughout the United States, from a variety of school settings, and with a variety of disabilities all achieved measurable gains in their phonemic awareness, word reading, and word writing skills" in the sixteen-week period of the study (Howell, Erickson, Stanger, & Wheaton, 2000, p. 13).

Guided Reading

Guided reading is a research-validated practice related to successful literacy development. In one-to-one situations or small reading groups, the teacher assists students in developing decoding and reading fluency by having students practice and have their errors corrected and remediated immediately.

The guided reading process can be supplemented by computers, which have students read along as words are highlighted on the screen, listening to the text on earphones, or clicking on unfamiliar words to hear them pronounced, defined, translated into another language, or segmented into syllables or phonemes. The Waterford Reading Program for primary age learners builds skills using a combined technology- and teacher-guided approach.

Steve Isaacs teaches a self-contained class of middle schoolers with mental retardation. He's found success with Reader Rabbit's Interactive Reading Journey, in which students progress through 40 small reading books, progressing as they demonstrate mastery of each book. Students not only read the book with the computer, but they must be able to read the book to Steve or his classroom aide. He notes: "Using computers for kids is so important. If it's just on paper, you lose a piece, and if it's just on the computer, you lose a piece. The computer utilizes a multi-sensory approach, providing both visual and auditory stimulation; for students with special needs, this is very beneficial" (Raia, 1997).

Student-Selected Reading

Among the issues teachers face in helping struggling readers is that success depends on frequent focused opportunities to read. When reading is difficult, students avoid doing it. When reading is pleasurable, students read more, thus learn more, and, even more importantly, read better. What can teachers do to make reading more enjoyable while they are learning the necessary foundation skills for reading success?

Programs such as Scholastic's WiggleWorks showcase the possibilities. This innovative program embodies the principles of universal design presented in Chapter 3. In WiggleWorks, highly engaging books, culturally resonant and age-appropriate, are presented in a hypertext medium. That means that students are empowered to make choices in how they read the book: Students select the speed, the voice, the scaffolds they prefer (pronunciation, definitions, language translations, read aloud, or student-read, etc).

For older students, Accelerated Reader offers highly engaging books on a variety of levels. Students take a quick reading assessment to pinpoint their reading level and diagnose reading comprehension needs and receive their suggested reading level. They then select from a variety of books at that level and move to the computer to take a multiple-choice comprehension test on that book. As their comprehension improves, the level increases, and new books are introduced. The combination of student choice, targeted reading levels, ongoing assessment and instant feedback, self-monitoring to review progress, and a reward/recognition system results in reluctant readers becoming motivated readers (Arnett, 2000).

Comprehension

Although programs like Accelerated Reader provide incentives for students to select and read books at their diagnosed reading level, and the tests provide a sort of structure to shape students' thinking about what they've read, these programs do not provide specific cues, strategies, or scaffolds for the comprehension process. In addition, the comprehension tests provide a mode of response that may be successful on standardized tests, but deep levels of comprehension are better assessed with more in-depth tools such as retelling or reflective writing.

Research on skills needed for successful reading comprehension has shown that students need the metacognitive skills of:

1. predicting what a passage or reading selection will be about before starting to read;
2. clarifying unfamiliar words through pronunciation prompts, explaining definitions, or using root word strategies to build meaning;
3. self-questioning for meaning (Who? What? When? Where? How? Why?) at both surface and deep levels;
4. paraphrasing and retelling the key points (Palinscar, 1984).

MacArthur and Haynes (1995) used a hypermedia software program to supplement a science textbook to assist secondary students with reading comprehension. The software featured speech synthesis for decoding and word recognition, an online glossary for definitions, and return links to the text passage. The software prompted students to use previewing, outlining, and self-questioning strategies. In their study, nine of the ten students performed significantly better on the comprehension test after using the software in addition to their textbook.

WRITING

Writing poses a variety of challenges for all students. First, students must generate ideas and organize them to produce a meaningful product. Second, they must use eye–hand coordination to either handwrite or keyboard their compositions. Third, students need to check their work for grammatical and spelling errors, edit the work, and submit a revised version for the teacher to review. Students with learning or cognitive disabilities rarely produce written work of a quality comparable to their general education peers and experience problems in virtually all areas of written expression. In addition, years of failure have convinced most students with learning disabilities that they have nothing worthwhile to share and do not see themselves as writers; frequently, these students associate writing assignments with anxiety and stress and try to avoid them whenever they can. The complexity of the process can be overwhelming for students and teachers alike. In what ways can the computer make the process efficient and effective for them?

Many teachers and parents who have experienced the power of word processing in their own lives assume that similar breakthroughs will automatically occur for their students. Others use word processing to do traditional drill-and-practice exercises on grammar and writing mechanics and are disappointed that technology is not a magic solution. Still others wonder about how to best combine the use of technology with writing process instruction, reading instruction, metacognitive teaching/learning strategies, cooperative learning/peer editing, and so forth.

Mind-Mapping

Mind-mapping, semantic mapping, clustering, idea generation and organization, all are terms that describe the first crucial stage in the writing process: the period during which students brainstorm their ideas for a composition and organize them into a sequence. The program used most frequently for this stage is Inspiration (grades 4 and up) and Kidspiration (grades K–3). This useful tool makes it easy for students to use words or pictures to generate a central idea, details, and an outline, in either a diagram or outline form, prior to beginning to write a first draft. Figure 5.1 contains a mind map done by a student preparing to write a book report on Stuart Little. Inspiration is also a wonderful tool for writing a lab report in science, a cause and effect analysis in social studies, or a Venn diagram in math.

Word Processing

Word processing has proven to be an extremely helpful tool for writers with and without disabilities. Using a tool to create, move, delete, insert, and otherwise edit text offers flexibility and power to teachers, parents, and students alike. Word processors can be used with keyboards that use the alphabetic (instead of the qwerty) order, adaptive keyboards like IntelliKeys, which provide different layouts or specially programmed keys with picture cues or to operate various aspects of the computer, and with speech synthesis, word prediction,

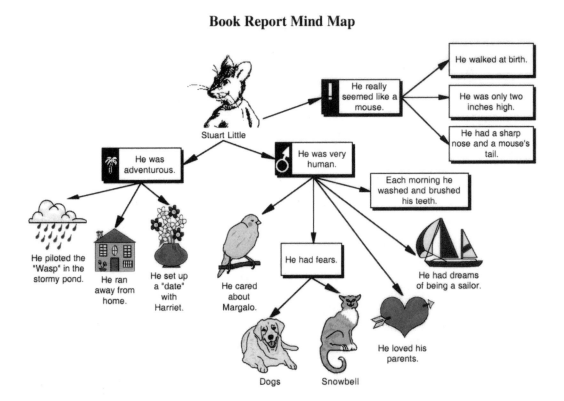

Book Report Mind Map

FIGURE 5.1   Book Report Mind Map

This diagram was created with Inspiration™, published by Inspiration Software, Inc.

or speech recognition (Ashton, 1999, 2000; MacArthur, Graham, Schwartz, & Schafer, 1995). Most word processors also offer spelling and grammar checkers.

Spelling and Grammar Checking.   Many students limit the qualities of the ideas and narratives they might write to the words they know how to spell. They also may limit their writing to simple declarative sentences because those are the sentences they know how to punctuate. Spell checkers can be effective in giving students greater confidence to express themselves more freely, especially when students have learned a strategy for using spell checkers effectively (Ashton, 1999). The most common problem with spelling checkers is that the student's spelling errors are not close enough to the correctly spelled word for the computer to guess what word the student is trying to spell. Ashton developed a learning strategy (CHECK) to help students become more fluent and more successful in using the spell checker to improve their written work. Table 5.1 shows the steps in the CHECK procedure. Students with learning disabilities need a strategy to use a spell checker effectively and efficiently (Lewis, 1996). Teachers should note, however, that spell checking has been shown to have an impact on the spelling difficulty but they will still need to provide direct instruction and practice to affect spelling performance.

Computer-assisted programs such as Spell It 3 have been used to help students learn and practice spelling rules, their use has no more impact on transfer to authentic written language tasks than paper-and-pencil drill programs.

Word prediction.   Word prediction programs were initially developed to reduce the number of keystrokes required for people with physical disabilities. When a user types the first letter of a word, a menu of word choices appears on the screen. The program attempts to "predict" the word, so that the user's keystrokes are reduced. For students whose spelling errors are so severe that a spell checker is not useful or practical, word prediction software, such as My Words or Co:Writer, may improve performance. MacArthur (1998) studied five students with severe spelling and writing difficulties using word recognition software. Four

TABLE 5.1   The CHECK Procedure

Check	Check the beginning sound of the word What other letter(s) could make that beginning sound? (Most spell checkers search for words beginning with the same letter.)
Hunt	Hunt for the correct consonants. Have you included all the consonants in the rest of the word?
Examine	Examine the vowels. What other vowel(s) could make the same sound?
Changes	Changes in suggested word lists may give hints. What words are being suggested? Is that the one you're looking for?
Keep	Keep repeating Steps 1 through 4. Need help? Try dictionaries and asking others for assistance.

From Spell CHECKing: Making Writing meaningful in the inclusive classroom by T. Ashton, *Teaching Exceptional Children, 32,* 1999, 24. Copyright by the Council for Exceptional Children. Reprinted with permission.

of five students improved their spelling, producing from 42 percent to 75 percent correctly spelled words. Results in other studies have been mixed, but what we know is:

1. Word prediction improves spelling and legibility for some students (differences in motivation, in attentiveness to the list of predicted words, or failure to select a correctly predicted word).
2. Word prediction software may be more helpful for some tasks than for others (using advanced or customized dictionaries may be helpful for some tasks).
3. Advances in word prediction programs may increase success for some students ("Flexible Spelling" in Co:Writer includes more flexible interpretations of what the student has tried to spell, such as "butfl" for *beautiful* (Fennema-Jansen, 2001).

For students whose expressive language is far superior to their written language, word prediction may be an excellent tool to maintain their motivation to complete writing assignments. Josh, aged 14, worked with Debbie Newton, an assistive technology specialist at the Center for Enabling Technology, a member of the Alliance for Technology Access. Debbie's initial recommendations were for three programs: Write Away, a word prediction program, Storybook Weaver Deluxe, and Spell It 3. They began with Write Away, and after only one session, Josh's confidence and interest in writing returned. Debbie found that Write Away helps students like Josh, because it enables him to avoid spelling mistakes, it reinforces the correct spelling of words, and it develops his writing skills (Niemann, 1996).

Adaptive keyboard/talking word processing. The adaptive keyboard is another tool developed for people with physical disabilities that has proven useful for a variety of other learning needs (such as English language learners, very young children, and students with learning disabilities). Using a larger keyboard or a keyboard in which programmable "keys" can be created of any size and paired with picture or word cues, students can write compositions just like their peers. Software such as IntelliTalk used with OverlayMaker and the IntelliKeys adds the benefits of speech synthesis to the adaptive keyboard for empowering students. Figure 5.2 provides an example of a writing overlay designed with Overlay Maker for IntelliKeys, and used with IntelliTalk. Not only does IntelliTalk "talk," but it also has a Picture Library and other features that capture students' engagement with the writing process.

Speech recognition. Another tool for word processing that is becoming more reasonable in price and more practical for widespread use is voice recognition software. For students with physical disabilities, fine motor difficulties, and written language challenges, such that none of the above options is adequate to compensate or bypass the disabilities, voice/speech recognition systems may provide another option. In Chapter 17, you can investigate the impact of speech recognition on environmental control for people with physical/communication disabilities. Voice recognition offers promise for students whose verbal linguistic skills are comparable to peers without disabilities in the area of written language.

Executives have long benefited from dictating written work. If the academic goal is one of transcribing ideas, summaries, narratives, and reflections, tools are now affordable,

Overlay for Use with IntelliTalk

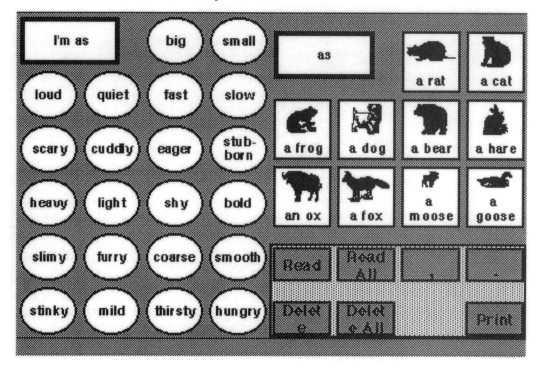

FIGURE 5.2   Overlay for Use with IntelliTalk

accessible, and practical to consider for students who have been limited by their lack of progress in other word-processing media.

Equally significantly, researchers are now finding that students who use speech recognition tools also may improve their word recognition, reading comprehension, and spelling (Higgins & Raskind, 2000). Both discrete speech recognition systems (in which the user must pronounce each word distinctly for the computer to process the sounds) and continuous speech recognition (in which the user can talk fluently, and the computer will continue to process the sounds) offer support to struggling readers. In discrete speech programs, the user is given a selection of choices for the word spoken to make corrections if the computer has heard it incorrectly on the same screen as the typing. In continuous speech, the user is switched to a correction screen after a phrase or sentence has been typed.

Translation.   For English language learners who are struggling with the interference of their native language as they respond to written language tasks, a Web site such as Alta Vista's Babel Fish (*www.babelfish.com*) may be useful.

MATH

Students who struggle in math have one or more of the following problems that may be helped by using a computer:

1. they don't have a conceptual understanding of the mathematical principle they are studying;
2. they have problems with short- or long-term memory and fluency of math facts that would enable them to solve problems more efficiently and effectively (automaticity);
3. they struggle with the language of word problems, which interferes with their selection of an appropriate algorithm or operation to solve the problem;
4. they have fine and gross motor problems that interfere with the organization of their work on paper.

Relatively few studies have been done that examine the impact of computer use on the understanding of mathematics principles by students with disabilities. One large-scale study of the impact of "The Adventures of Jasper Woodbury" on students with disabilities found significant increases in attitudinal and problem-solving measures (Pellegrino et al., 1991). In a study of contextualized problem solving with 36 students in which they watched a videodisc and then generated and solved the challenges, results showed significant improvement pre- to post-testing. In addition, the ability to transfer these skills to new problems requiring different mathematical procedures was also promising (Bottge & Hasselbring, 1993).

The development of fluency in math facts is an important component in success in math classes and in developing the confidence to attempt more complex math problems. The effectiveness of computer-assisted instruction has been supported in a number of studies, although the design of the software is strongly related to outcomes. Effective software design features included a small instructional set of unknown items, controlled response time, and immediate feedback. Neither bonus feedback nor game reinforcement within the

FIGURE 5.3   Assistive technology increases access to the general education math curriculum.

TABLE 5.2 Math Software

TITLE	PUBLISHER
Mighty Math Series	Edmark *www.edmark.com*
Millie's Math House	Edmark
Accelerated Math	Renaissance *www.renaissance.com*
Representing Fractions Combining and Breaking Apart Numbers Grouping and Place Value	Tenth Planet *www.tenthplanet.com*
Geometric superSupposer	Sunburst *www.sunburst.com*
Number Concepts 1 & 2 MathPad & MathPad Plus Intellimathics	IntelliTools *www.intellitools.com*
James Discovers Math	Broderbund *www.broderbund.com*

programs resulted in higher achievement; in fact, such features reduced the amount of time available for practice (Fitzgerald & Koury, 1996). Math software that includes the useful design features is provided in Table 5.2.

SOCIAL STUDIES

Social studies is frequently an area in which students with disabilities are welcomed into the inclusive classroom, with a variety of hands-on activities in which students with multiple abilities and challenges can participate as they learn about their world. On the other hand, social studies is also the place where the difficulty of textbooks interferes with students' participation in the classroom. Rose and Fernlund (1997, p. 162) suggest five questions to evaluate the use of technology in social studies instruction:

- Does the technology resource help promote *meaningful* social studies?
- Does the technology promote social studies that are integrated into other subject areas?
- Does the technology acknowledge *value-based* social studies?
- Does the technology provide social studies instruction that is *challenging*?
- In what ways can technology be helpful in this important subject area?
- Does technology actively engage students in significant social studies content?

In Chapter 2, you explored the use of databases, spreadsheets, and presentation software; in Chapter 8, you will explore Webquest to teach students research skills using the Internet, so important in social studies. Other ways that technology supports social studies instruction are:

1. simulations
2. mapmaking
3. time lines

Software that teachers have found effective in teaching social studies is listed in Table 5.3.

Simulations

Simulations give students a chance to experience the consequences of their decisions. The SimCity series focuses on the consequences of economic and environmental decisions; Oregon Trail and Amazon Trail take students back in time to incredible adventures on a journey in which they build knowledge about a different world through using the tools and resources available in another time.

Decisions, Decisions (Tom Snyder) presents students with critical situations drawn from history or contemporary issues. Taking on the roles of leaders and decision makers, students learn how to gather and review information, discuss options, and take action.

Mapmaking

For students whose fine motor skills get in the way of producing legible and attractive maps, tools such as Mapmaker's Toolkit is a wonderfully empowering tool. Students and teachers can produce historical or current maps, with different layers (boundaries, rivers, geographic features, cities, etc.) that can be printed or added to a Web page. Another type of program lets students use a drawing tool to create a contour map and see a three-dimensional view of the terrain (Roblyer & Edwards, 2000). For younger students, Neighborhood Map Machine introduces them to concepts of map design and geography skills, such as compass directions, scale, and grid coordinates.

Time Lines

One way of understanding history is to look at the relationship of events to the time period in which they occurred. Teachers and students can highlight scientific achievements,

TABLE 5.3 Social Studies Software

Carmen Sandiego series	The Learning Company
Where in the USA?	
Where in the World?	
Carmen Sandiego Jr. Detective	
Oregon Trail	
Amazon Trail	
TimeLiner	Tom Snyder
Decisions, Decisions	"
Neighborhood Map Machine	"
Map Maker's Toolkit	

geographic discoveries, or their own personal history by using a time line program such as TimeLiner 4.0 to select a time period and annotate the events.

SCIENCE

Most students with IEPs have had goals and objectives that addressed skills of reading, writing, and math. However, with emphasis on participation in the general education curriculum (and assessment), more focus on science learning across all service delivery settings from general to special education classrooms is expected (Anderson & Anderson, 2000). Mastropieri, Scruggs, and Magnusen (1999) have found that students with disabilities learn more when teachers use a hands-on, activities-based science curriculum and materials. Software programs that have been successful in many classrooms are listed in Table 5.4.

Life Science

Anderson and Anderson (2000) suggest that a unit on fossils and archeology can be supplemented by Message in a Fossil (Edunetics). In this program, students see videoclips of actual archeologists with suggestions of how to collect and categorize the fossils they locate and keep a journal of what they find. Hands-on activities can include real archeology digs with plots of ground or plastic trays with buried objects to count, classify, and draw. Shannon Webber (2001) used Dinosaur Ice Cream Cups by Schaums in which dinosaur cookies are buried in different layers of ice cream. Students must identify the dinosaur as well as the layer (fudge? sherbet?) in which the cookie was found. A word search activity at *www.quia.com/ws/102879.html* reinforces the vocabulary.

Keeping track of data can be done with programs such as The Graph Club (Tom Snyder) and The Cruncher (Davidson) (see Chapter 2). Trudy's Time and Place House (Edmark) helps students learn how to use grids and coordinates to locate items they've found.

Very young students will appreciate the "If I Were" activity (Lachina, 1998). The IntelliKeys and a specially designed overlay from the Activity Exchange at IntelliTools enable a student to select a real or imaginary creature and write a story about the creature, with a description of various aspects of the creature's appearance and diet. The student can select an appropriate voice to read the story aloud.

TABLE 5.4   Science Software

Sammy's Science House	Edmark
Thinkin' Science ZAP!	"
virtual labs	
The Great Ocean Rescue	Tom Snyder Productions
The Great Solar System Rescue	"
Rainforest Researchers	"
Science Seekers	"
Voyage of the Mimi	Sunburst

Simulations in science, such as Rainforest Researchers (Tom Snyder), provide students with a cooperative format to investigate a real-life problem. Using video, resource materials, and the software, students reach their own conclusions and get feedback along the way.

Physical Science

Just as Rainforest Researchers provides a highly engaging investigation of life science issues, The Great Solar System Rescue and The Great Ocean Rescue (also by Tom Snyder) present students with a situation they must solve in outer space. By learning about the solar system, students, in cooperative groups, solve a problem. Students watch a videoclip, make a decision, and then the computer plays a different videoclip, depending on the outcome (Docterman, 1997).

Simulations in physical science offer students the opportunity to do potentially hazardous chemistry experiments without the explosions. In Virtual Labs: Light and Virtual Labs: Electricity (Edmark), students do experiments and simulations using lasers, optical tools, and electrical devices—safely! For younger students (grades 3–6), Thinkin' Science ZAP! helps students practice thinking and problem solving while they build scientific understanding.

Earth Science

Sammy's Science House (Edmark) introduces young children to classifying, sequencing, and weather, including temperature, wind, and precipitation. These activities can be followed by graphing and creating spreadsheets of weather data collected over days and weeks, culminating in charts using KidPix Studio Deluxe, which combines pictures. ClarisWorks for Kids has prepared science activities that teachers and students will find useful.

Probeware

Probeware consists of hardware devices (probes) and software that processes or analyzes the information (thermometers, sensors to measure heat, voltage, pulse rate, Ph, etc.). Using these tools, students can conduct experiments on topics of interest to them and learn about the scientific method of testing hypotheses.

Videodiscs/Barcode/Authoring

Teachers can use videodiscs and barcode scanners to do hands-on experiments supported by film and photographs. Newton's Apple (PBS) provides videodiscs of its catalog of television shows and software for students to conduct their own experiments, and teachers can use these innovative, engaging lessons with students of all ability levels. Teachers can use software such as HyperStudio to design lessons which use the bar code and point students directly to the appropriate film clip or photograph.

TABLE 5.5   Teacher/Student Practice Tools—All Subject Areas

TITLE	URL ADDRESS	NOTES
Crossword puzzles and word searches	*http://puzzlemaker.school.discovery.com/*	Teachers and students can create puzzles and games on any curriculum area and at any difficulty level
Electronic Timeline	*www.ldresources.com*	Teachers and students can create time lines to describe any period in history
Drill and practice games	*www.quia.com* *http://mathforum.com*	Games are organized by subject and skill, arranged by difficulty

SKILL DEVELOPMENT TOOLS FOR TEACHERS, STUDENTS, AND PARENTS

Wissick (2000) notes that purchasing software for drill and practice is expensive and may be repetitive for students who need lots of practice opportunities to develop automaticity. She suggests that teachers develop "toolboxes" of Web sites that can provide inexpensive, adaptable solutions to subject area practice. Her own Web sites, *www.ed.sc.edu/caw/toolboxla.html* and *www.ed.sc.edu/caw/toolboxmath.html,* are wonderful resources.

Teachers may also want to do their own searches periodically for these teacher/student tools. Table 5.5 provides some places to begin.

STUDENT ACTIVITIES

1. Interview three teachers about the types of software they use with students. What criteria do they use to select software? What is the percentage of their use of drill-and-practice software compared to other applications presented in this book?

2. Select a piece of software that you have never used and try it out with a student (go to a publisher Web site and use a demo version of the program or order a program for a 45-day free trial). List three strengths and three limitations of the software from your experience of working with the student. Interview the student to determine the student's perceptions of the software's benefits and limitations.

3. For each of the subject areas you teach, make a list of software (from the chapter and from your own experience) that might enhance student access to the general education curriculum.

REFERENCES

Anderson, K., & Anderson, C. (2000). Science software and activities for all children. *Special Education Technology Practice, 2*(1), 10–14.

Arnett, P. (2000). Mastering reading & writing with technology. *Media & Methods, 37*(1), 10.

Ashton, T. (1999). Spell CHECKing: Making writing meaningful in the inclusive classroom. *Teaching Exceptional Children 32*(2), 24–27.

Ashton, T. (2000) Making technology work in the inclusive classroom: A Spell CHEKing strategy for students with learning disabilities. [On-line]. Available: *http://www.ldonline.org/ld_indepth/technology/ashton_spellcheck.html*

Bottge, B., & Hasselbring, T. (1993). A comparison of two approaches for teaching complex, authentic mathematics problems to adolescents in remedial math classes. *Exceptional Children, 59*(6), 556–566.

Docterman, D. (1997). *Great teaching in the one-computer classroom.* Watertown, MA: Tom Snyder Productions.

Earle, J. (1998). Fast ForWord: Is the hype justified? *TECH-NJ, 9*(1), 1–3.

Fennema-Jansen, S. (2001). Measuring effectiveness: Technology to support writing. *Special Education Technology Practice, 1*(1), 16–22.

Fitzgerald, G., & Koury, K. (1996). Empirical advances in technology-assisted instruction for students with mild and moderate disabilities. *Journal of Research on Computing in Education, 28,* 526–553.

Higgins, E., & Raskind, M. (2000). Speaking to read: The effects of continuous vs. discrete speech recognition systems on the reading and spelling of children with learning disabilities. *Journal of Special Education Technology, 15*(1), 19–30.

Howell, R., Erickson, K., Stanger, C., & Wheaton, J. (2000). Evaluation of a computer-based program on the reading performance of first grade students with potential for reading failure. *Journal of Special Education Technology, 15*(4), 5–14.

Lachina, K. (1998). *If I Were.* IntelliTools Activity Exchange. Petaluma: IntelliTools.

Lewis, R. (1996). *Enhancing the writing skills of students with learning disabilities through technology.* Funded project. U.S. Department of Education, Office of Special Education Programs.

MacArthur, C. (1998). From illegible to understandable: How word recognition and speech synthesis can help. *Teaching Exceptional Children, 30*(6) 66–71.

MacArthur, C., Graham, S., Schwartz, S., & Schafer, W. (1995). Evaluation of a writing instruction model that integrated a process approach, strategy instruction, and word processing. *Learning Disability Quarterly, 18,* 278–291.

MacArthur, C., & Haynes, J. (1995). Student assistant for learning from text (SALT): A hypermedia reading aid. *Journal of Learning Disabilities, 28*(3), 150–159.

Mastropieri, M., Scruggs, T., & Magnusen, M. (1999). Activities-oriented science instruction for students with disabilities. *Remedial and Special Education, 22,* 240–249.

Niemann, D. (1996). Word prediction makes the difference: Learning disabilities in middle school. *TECH-NJ, 8*(1), 1–2.

Palinscar, A. (1984). *Reciprocal teaching: Field evaluations in remedial and content-area reading.* Paper presented at the annual meeting of the American Educational Research Association, Washington, DC.

Pellegrino, J., Hickey, D., Heath, A., Rewey, K., Vye, N., & Cognition and Techology Group at Vanderbilt. (1991). Assessing the outcomes of an innovative instructional program: The 1990–91 implementation of the "Adventures of Jasper Woodbury" (Tech. Rep. No 91-111). Nashville, TN: Vanderbilt University, Learning Technology Center.

Raia, O. (1997). Computers help students and their teacher at Montclair Middle School. *TECH-NJ, 8*(2), 1–3.

Roblyer, M., & Edwards, J. (2000). *Integrating educational technology into teaching.* Upper Saddle River, NJ: Merrill.

Rose, S., & Fernlund, P. (1997). Using technology for powerful social studies learning. *Social Education, 61*(3), 160–166.

Tallal, P. (1995). Evaluating new training programs for language impairment. *ASHA, 39,* 12.

Webber, S. (2001). *Dinosaur lesson plan.* Unpublished paper for SPED 346C, California State University, Chico.

Wissick, C. (2000). Quickstarts: Drill and practice Web style. *Special Education Technology Practice. 2*(3), 37–39.

CHAPTER SIX

DESIGNING INTENSIVE INDIVIDUAL INTERVENTIONS
Disability-Specific Considerations

Many technology applications are useful across disability conditions. However, some applications are more usually associated with particular disabilities. In this chapter, those unique applications are listed and described. Many teachers who work with students who have specific disabilities may be interested in reading about applications and examples of technology related to a particular disability. In this chapter, you can explore ideas for using technology to respond to particular needs. Case studies of students in this chapter help bring the ideas of this book to life, illustrating the benefits of technology for individual students.

CHAPTER GOALS

By the end of this chapter, you will be able to:

1. describe the benefits of a particular technology to address the needs of a student with a specific category of disability;
2. compare the uses of technology across disability categories;
3. see the benefits of technology through the eyes of students and families;
4. identify technology applications that will benefit students with whom you work.

VISUAL IMPAIRMENTS

General computer applications for individuals who have low vision include (Kelly, 2000):

- large print for video displays and printers
- speech synthesis/screen readers
- fax
- electronic messaging
- verbal description of video and television
- accessible Web sites appropriate for screen readers

For students who are blind, the following technology options are considered essential:

- speech synthesis,
- hard-copy Braille
- refreshable Braille (paperless)
- text to Braille and Braille to text
- fax
- electronic messaging
- verbal description for video and television
- accessible Web sites appropriate for screen readers

In *Tech-NJ,* published by The College of New Jersey, Theresa Lupo (1997) describes the impact of technology on Serena, a student with visual impairments.

As a second-grader, Serena learned touch typing and began to operate an Apple IIe computer that was equipped with a screen reader, a speech synthesizer and a Braille printer. Her teacher printed spelling lists, writing assignments, and math lessons for Serena and her classmates simultaneously by connecting the computer to both the Braille and standard printers. The classroom aide also used the system to print written materials such as announcements, Valentine's Day cards, the program for the school play, and the teacher's grading comments, which she would staple to Serena's work.

The following year, Serena began changing classes and needed a more portable method of writing. While her classmates learned handwriting, Serena learned the handwriting of the blind using a slate and stylus. This simple device enables individuals to produce Braille by hand.

At this time her parents and teachers began to consider high-tech options. They decided on a laptop computer with screen reading software and a refreshable Braille display (TeleSensory). A laptop computer from Compaq was selected because Serena already knew the QWERTY keyboard, and having a regular screen display would enable her teachers, who could not read Braille, to follow along as she wrote. Serena's mother also thought that a laptop would be easier to integrate in the future as Serena's needs changed. "I was excited to get a computer. It was cool to have something new to use," Serena added.

"Probably the biggest problem we encountered was getting all the components to work together. I think that anyone who has a complicated computer set-up will have that problem, and most blind people do. It took us a long time to get everything to talk to each other. I expect that that will happen again as we add more things," Carol stated. Cost was also a factor in the selection process. The laptop and screen-reading software were donated by a local service organization. Both Serena and her mother received computer training through the New Jersey Commission for the Blind and Visually Impaired. Equipment purchased by the Commission follows children to whatever school or program they attend, and therefore does not need to be included in the I.E.P. The school district has paid for the Braille printer.

Serena uses low-tech items provided by the Commission for the Blind and Visually Impaired, such as a Braille ruler, Braille versions of student textbooks, a talking calculator, a handheld talking dictionary (*Franklin Language Master 6000 SE*), and a Braille dictionary. "With the talking dictionary she can quickly look up the definitions, but she also needs to use the Braille dictionary to learn the syllabication and pronunciation markings. You can't do that unless you can see it right under your fingers. We felt that it was important for Serena to learn to do both. The Braille dictionary stays at school. It's definitely not portable; it takes up about 20 feet of shelf space!" Carol exclaimed.

She continued, "I believe that one of the skills that Serena needs is to know when to switch to different items to accomplish different tasks. There are times when she likes to use one thing and times when she likes to use another. For reports, she might Braille her first draft, check it, then write her second draft on the computer. A lot of sighted people would do that—hand-write our first draft, then type it on the computer. Sometimes she writes on the computer, then Brailles a copy for herself. The talking computer makes writing easier because she can check and correct her own work. Before, if she made a typo, a sighted person would have to read it and correct it. It has helped to increase her independence." "I use my laptop for homework sometimes. I also like writing stories on it, just for fun," Serena added.

Next year, Serena will begin 7th grade in the Junior High and will need to have a completely portable writing device. To facilitate this transition, she and her mother obtained a list of all the resources and goals in the Junior High. In March, they took this list to the International Braille and Technology Center for the Blind in Baltimore, Maryland where they checked out extensive displays of technology and Braille-producing instruments.

They were able to select adaptive equipment that will allow Serena to access all the software and equipment she will encounter at school. Serena and her mother decided on a *Braille Lite* (Blazie), a small, portable note-taker with 6-key Braille input and a 40-cell refreshable Braille display. This will enable Serena to take notes in class and print them later. They were also able to preview other technology which serves the needs of blind people. There are several items that Serena doesn't use yet like scanners for reading books. These would allow her direct access to print. Eventually, I'm sure, she'll begin using those.

HEARING IMPAIRMENTS

For students who are deaf or hard of hearing, the following technology tools are considered essential (Kelly, 2000):

- telecommunications
- captioned television and videos
- fax
- language development and computer-assisted instruction for reading and writing skills
- C-Print (a hearing operator who transcribes a spoken lecture on a PC, which uses a combination of words for a word processor and abbreviations in a type of productivity processor, enabling the note-taker to transcribe words as rapidly as they are spoken.

Kristin Anderson (2001) has described how assistive technology (an FM system) has improved the learning experience for a child with severe hearing loss.

Kevin is a bright six-year-old in first grade. As a toddler, Kevin had numerous ear infections that caused severe hearing loss in both of his ears. At four years old, he was placed in a Deaf/Hard of Hearing Pre-Kindergarten class, where he became fluent in sign language. When Kevin was five, he received digital hearing aids. These technically advanced hearing aids dramatically improved his hearing.

Kevin's IEP team met and decided that he would be successful if he were integrated in a general education first-grade class. An interpreter was to sit next to him and cue him when he couldn't hear the teacher. Kevin resented the stigma of the interpreter, who followed him wherever he went. By the fourth week of his first-grade experience, Kevin was completely ignoring the interpreter. Kevin also became easily angered from his inability to hear in the classroom because there was so much background noise. Kevin eventually admitted that he "just wanted to hear like all the other kids in the class."

The IEP team decided to try an FM system, with speakers in the classroom to amplify the teacher's voice. Kevin was taught how to attach the FM system to his hearing aids, turn on the system, and keep the battery pack safe in his pocket. Likewise, the first-grade teacher was taught how to operate the battery pack and microphone that she wore.

Virtually overnight this assistive technology changed Kevin's schooling experience. He no longer became easily angered because he can actually hear the teacher. Much to Kevin's relief, there isn't an interpreter signer who follows him around the classroom anymore. He has been making significant progress in his academic achievement as well. Most of all, Kevin's frustration level has decreased tremendously. He is more social and happy as a result (Anderson, 2001).

PHYSICAL DISABILITIES

Some of the essential technology for people with physical disabilities includes (Langone, 2000):

- environmental modifications for placement of keyboard, monitor, or both
- keyboard adaptations such as keylocks and keyguards
- software to simulate mouse movement
- alternative keyboards, such as IntelliKeys
- software to allow the user to control computer functions such as Ke:nx, with which the user can use a single switch
- environmental controls using switches

John is eleven years old and attends school in a program for medically fragile students who are, for the most part, nonverbal. John has cerebral palsy; he is quadriplegic; he has a severe seizure disorder to the degree that surgery was required to remove part of his brain in order to get the seizures under a reasonable amount of control (Storey, 2001). The classroom teachers provide total care for the students there, including diapering and feeding. John seems to be a content boy for the most part and expresses pleasure in things by cooing. The surgery performed on his brain greatly altered his affect, however. Before the surgery he was a lively, smiley boy and since the surgery his personality is very flat. He doesn't laugh or smile much and he doesn't cry or express discontent much. And yet, at the same time, he is aware of his surroundings and interactions with people and responds occasionally with a smile or coo.

The goals for these students are primarily social and physical. The majority of John's IEP focuses on positioning to make his body more limber and keep his muscles active. He is to use the stander, beanbag, side lier, and prone wedge throughout the day. His social goals include music, books, art, and sensory stimulation. Technology for John focuses on the Ablenet Switch Box, which engages him in his environment and improves the quality of his life.

The Ablenet Switch Box is an electronic box to which any electrical device can be connected. John uses this switch box to make his own food for breakfast. Because he can easily aspirate, all of John's food needs to be blended. The teacher connects the blender to one end of the switch box and a large round, red switch button called the "Big Mac" to the other end. When John hits the Big Mac, the blender is turned on. There is a dial on the switch box, which allows the teacher to control the amount of time the blender stays on and then it shuts off automatically. In this way, John prepares his own food and becomes more active in his daily life. A similar technique is used for him to sharpen pencils, shred paper, and operate other small cooking appliances.

The class has several different kinds of switch buttons, including voice-activated, and buttons that record human voice and repeat the recorded message when pressed. Some students are using these successfully to indicate "yes" or "no" during academic lessons. Another of John's goals is using the switch button to communicate back and forth between the parent and the teacher daily. John can't tell his mother if he had a bowel movement or how many seizures he had that day so the teacher and mother send a switch button back and forth in his backpack to communicate these things. The teacher records the information on the switch and sends it home with John so that, when his mother asks him how his day was, he pushes the switch to sound the recording that will let her know. In that way, he is more involved in his own day.

The communication goal in John's IEP states that he "will activate a Big Mac switch at home to tell one activity at school and will activate the switch at school to tell one activity from home at least one time per week with partial physical prompting by May, 2001,…[and] will activate the switch to say "yes" one time in answer to a question during story related activities in school setting 10% of the time with partial assistance or independently by May, 2001."

DEVELOPMENTAL DISABILITIES

People with moderate to severe mental retardation may benefit from the following features of technology (Okolo, 2000; Wehmeyer, 1999):

- computer-assisted instruction that breaks skills down into smaller steps, with unlimited opportunities for repetition and practice with feedback;
- simulations of situations in which students can practice social skills, life skills, and vocational skills prior to transferring the skills to real-life situations (in which the risks or logistics might reduce practice opportunities);
- augmentative communication devices with communication boards with pictures and words, so that students can communicate desires, requests, social interactions, and so on.

Alice is eighteen years old and attends a county program for students with severe disabilities on a high school campus (Vazquez, 2001). She was born with a disorder of the 18th Chromosome, which influenced development in the major life areas of cognition, language, social-emotional, motor, and adaptive functioning.

FIGURE 6.1   Alice uses technology to communicate.

Alice's parents requested an augmentative communication device. The IEP team agreed that this could be beneficial to her. She uses a MessageMate by Words+. The device has four levels with 40 buttons on each level. The overlays are created on the computer by using the program, *Boardmaker.* To activate the device, she pushes a button with an icon in order to retrieve a recorded word or phrase. She uses it spontaneously in conversation along with verbalizations. One difficulty with Alice and her MessageMate is that she frequently perseverates when vocalizing and when using her MessageMate.

Alice is generally happy and compliant. She takes care of her MessageMate well. Initially, she did not like the device; three years later, it has become part of her. "A" remembers the levels and locations of icons that are her favorites. She is able to access some words or phrases without changing overlays. This helps the fluency of her communication.

Alice uses this technology in all settings. She wears it at home and school. She uses it to initiate conversations, usually "My name is Alice. What's your name?" (She may do this over and over again, even if she knows the person's name.) Parents say that she uses it on the telephone, especially when talking to grandparents. During our opening meeting, she used it for sharing, to lead the pledge of allegiance, tell the date, and say what yesterday, today, and tomorrow are. She uses the device to order meals at restaurants and to specify food preferences at home. She uses the MessageMate to tell others of her needs and desires.

Each year Alice's overlays have been changed or modified. It has been a collaborative effort, but mostly as a result of requests initiated by the parents. The parents designed the last set of overlays. With each change, Alice needs to relearn the location of old icons and the meaning and locations of the new icons.

Alice's current IEP goal in regards to the MessageMate is to "learn the locations of icons that have been moved and additional icons/words that have been added to her MessageMate with 70% accuracy by 1/02, as determined by review of data on tracking sheets." Alice's increasing skills will improve her ability to communicate socially as well as academically. She is studying the device in class by doing a drill-and-practice exercise involving the location of eight items at random on each level. Her responses are tallied on data tracking sheets. She also sits on her bed at home and presses the buttons, studying and memorizing the locations of icons and their phrases.

The use of the MessageMate has increased Alice's verbal output as well as her overall communication level. Her participation in a broad spectrum of activities both at home and school has increased.

AUTISM

Because students with autism frequently feel more comfortable with computer technology than in personal communication situations, the following technology tools may be of great benefit to families and teachers:

- augmentative communication devices
- computer-assisted instruction
- simulations for social skills and life skills training

Cynthia Bott (1998) wrote this case study about Andrew for *Tech-NJ,* a technology journal.

Andrew is an energetic five year old with autism who loves Mother Goose, singing any Disney song, and kisses. He attends a private school designed for students with autism. As coordinator of the early childhood program, I see Andrew on a daily basis and have the opportunity to observe his interactions with his peers and teachers.

Andrew does not speak. He does make efforts at sign language and verbal approximations, but only upon request and rarely spontaneously. Andrew is agile and has excellent fine motor control. Cognitively, he exhibits splinter skills in academic areas. He has a list of over 100 sight words that he can identify, and he can sequence numbers past 25, yet he cannot retrieve objects by name or understand the simplest abstract concept. Andrew also has great difficulty sitting still for longer than three seconds at a time, making it even harder for his teachers to assess his knowledge.

Andrew's family purchased an augmentative system to aid his communication. Prior to this, he had been using a Picture Exchange Communication System with about 50 computer-generated pictures representing Andrew's most common needs and wants. While this helped alleviate some of Andrew's frustration, it did not provide him with a voice, and it also became difficult to include all of his increasing needs. At a language seminar, his parents became introduced to a high-tech system called the DynaMyte (Sentient Systems Technology), a small, hand-held unit which they purchased with help from their insurance company.

Andrew's DynaMyte has been amazing in what it has done for him. It is a square, gray box, about 7 inches on each side, and 2 inches deep. It has a touch screen, with a protective, plastic lid that flips open and shut. Andrew's parents had a customized carrying case designed with padding and a longer strap than originally supplied to protect it from accidentally being dropped. This enables Andrew to carry around the system himself, without his teachers and parents being fearful of any damage he might do.

The DynaMyte has a memory card installed, and it is simply programmed to meet individual needs. The speech therapist and Andrew's mother attended a special training session to enable them to program his system and troubleshoot any problems that may arise. When looking at the touch screen, one sees three rows containing icons of folders (four in each row). Each folder represents a different category, which when touched changes the screen to a specific overlay of pictures/letters/words appropriate to that category.

There is a blank bar across the top of that overlay, and when Andrew presses the icons he wants, they appear in that bar in the order they are pressed. When his sentence is complete, Andrew needs to touch that bar, and the system reads aloud the entire sentence. For example, if Andrew wants to ask for a pretzel, he touches the food folder on the master page. This calls up the food page, with an assortment of phrases and food symbols pictured on cells. He then can touch the "I want" "pretzel" "please" cells and they will appear in the bar that runs across the top of the food page. Then, with a touch on that bar, the DynaMyte reads the sentence in its entirety. The memory card installed in the system has an extensive vocabulary, and if a word is programmed in that the computer does not recognize, it will read it phonetically. All the programs that Andrew needs are contained within the system—no additional hardware or software is needed, just the ability to set-up each folder so that it contains individualized items.

Currently, Andrew has several folders programmed into his system that enable him to communicate his needs both at home and at school. His pages include: food, drinks, school (with circle time vocabulary, early learning concepts, etc.), music (with a "sing me" cell and various song titles), reinforcer items (videos, computer game titles), letters (arranged in a "qwerty" keyboard format), and home (family names, book and movie titles, etc.). Prior to receiving the system, he was evaluated for his ability to move from the master page through several different folders. Andrew's success at that time was incredible, and to see him currently move from page to page with no difficulty finding what he desires is amazing.

The DynaMyte goes with Andrew everywhere. At home, he apparently takes it to bed. The system has become his voice, and he truly understands that concept. At school, it sits on his desk within reach, or next to him during group activities. His spontaneous language has increased dramatically, since now he knows people understand what he is requesting—his family often hear the voice asking for items throughout the house without any questions having been asked. It has been eye-opening to his teachers to realize that when they present Andrew with a choice of what they think he wants, and he turns around and voices a completely different opinion, they were wrong. For example, the teachers may try to reinforce Andrew's good behavior with a choice of pretzels or soda, and he will use his computer to say he wants to listen to music! Andrew has also demonstrated a hidden phonetic ability that we might not have discovered for some time had it not been for his letters page. When his computer was first being programmed and he did not have all the words in folders yet, he would go to his letters page and "spell" out words using phonics and invented spelling. This also made us realize just how much more he was absorbing from his reading programs than we had originally thought.

The one behavioral issue we are discovering about Andrew now that he has a voice is his desire to perseverate on various topics—usually his favorite videos or songs. He will either type in a title several times before hitting the speak bar (so his teacher will hear "Mother Goose" spoken five times in a row), or he will repeatedly ask for the same item over a long duration, ignoring all other pages on the system. While we are addressing this issue from a behavioral standpoint, we are, at the same time, glad that he now has the communication capabilities to do this!

Because Andrew's fine motor control is refined, he can use a clear point to touch each individual cell, and these cells are small in size. This will allow room for expansion of the system's vocabulary in the future. I would like to see Andrew become more involved in the community and use his system to communicate to people other than those in his immediate circle. As a five year old with some behavioral issues that still need to be addressed, his access to the community is limited. His DynaMyte, however, is the first step to breaking down that barrier. He is less frustrated about communicating than before, and the system has a clear enough voice output that the general public will be able to understand his requests. Andrew is a different child because of his DynaMyte, and he will be able to go so much farther than many of his teachers ever realized.

EMOTIONAL DISTURBANCE

Students who have severe behavior problems or emotional disturbance may benefit from the use of technology in several ways:

- The computer can help students and teachers discover hidden interests or talents that can be used to re-direct unacceptable to difficult behaviors.

- Computer time can serve as an activity reinforcer to help students engage in more productive behavior during class.
- As with students who have learning disabilities, the computer can serve as an organizing tool to help students keep track of their work.
- The private and anonymous features of communicating on the Internet may provide students with an avenue for communication and reflection.

Danny is a fourth-grade student functioning initially at the first-grade level academically in all tested areas with severe emotional disturbance (Mullin, 2001). Danny's parents transferred him from a nearby non-technology-using classroom to Todd Mullins' learning center class when they saw him falling deeper into a pattern of failure. Danny suffers from a cyclic disorder of mood with one side bright and eager to learn, and the other side dark, angry and defiant. Danny has developed the sense that he is artistic and uses this to balance out his decreased performance in other areas.

The major goal for Danny is to transform his educational experience. The teachers want to engage his genuine interests and abilities and eventually tie into the regular subjects of math, reading and writing. By utilizing a wide variety of programs, his teacher notices where Danny's interests are. These interests are used as motivators for Danny to maintain his behavior and participation in school.

Technology is the major vehicle. Many of the programs are highly interactive in a way that allows Danny to explore *on his own terms*. This ease of exploration bleeds into nontechnology time with Danny.

The first program to really grab Danny's attention was Painter (Meta Creations). This is a commercial/professional quality painting program that allows the user to make many, many choices, to apply and experiment with these choices, and to observe, self-assess, and then modify those choices instantly. Along with Painter, several math programs, like Math Blaster, Turbo Math, Math Rabbit, and Web sites like *multiplication.com* give Danny a multitude of choices to select from, each with choices as to type and difficulty level. Again, the major idea is to first, and throughout the process, build confidence and stability.

In Painter, Danny initially created samples of color. That led to more complex expressions of color in relationship to other colors. He then began to explore various effects applied to his paintings. Soon he discovered the pattern catalogues from which he could select and paint, creating stunning landscapes and scenes that were breathtaking. Gone was the dark, incapable, and unproductive side! Awakened was the creative and excited learner!

In Crystal, Danny is competing with his own top score to achieve mastery with a competitive challenge of rounding-up moving and evasive elements on the screen with increasing skill. He has long since passed the highest scores previously on the program history and has established himself as "champion of the hill."

In Turbo Math Danny answers addition and subtraction problems with increasing skill. His ultimate reward is one of the higher motivational programs, along with learning math skills that definitely carry over into the nontechnology classes.

Danny will probably be a lifelong user of technology. The quirks of personality and disability that cause social problems are sidestepped through his use of technology as his medium for learning. It represents freedom for Danny, freedom to win and succeed like never before!

Danny's parents cannot believe the difference they see in him! His thinking has clarified to the degree that this once dull, unhappy boy is now playing chess with increasing skill, after only seven months! They see Danny progressing at a rate they thought impossible.

LEARNING DISABILITIES

For students with learning disabilities, technology is essential in a variety of ways (Okolo, 2000; Zhang, 2000):

- CDs, DVDs to support teaching and deliver instruction in different modes;
- electronic books, which scaffold the reading process with pronunciation, definitions, and prompted comprehension activities;
- word processors with spelling and grammar checkers;
- word processors with word prediction, such as Co-Writer;
- speech synthesis and word processors;
- idea processors such as Inspiration and TimeLiner;
- organizational tools such as a Palm Pilot;
- reference tools (electronic encyclopedias).

Joey is a fifth-grade student with learning disabilities (Smith, 2001). He participates in a blended program of resource specialist services, a self-contained special day classroom, and a Title I program for low-income students at risk. Teachers in all these programs collaborate to serves students with and without Individualized Education Programs.

Joey is a very capable and eager student, but he has a fine motor deficit. Joey finds it very difficult and time-consuming to write. He needs a lot of space to create his letters, which usually come out illegible. Because simple tasks become frustrating for Joey, he uses an Alpha Smart Pro to type his assignments. He keeps a daily planner with all of his homework assignments written in on the appropriate day. Joey has trouble staying in the small squares but tries his best to handwrite these assignments in the given format. He also handwrites the rough drafts of all of his papers and completes his math sheets in handwriting.

Using the Alpha Smart Pro is one way for him to get his thoughts out quickly. When he must concentrate so hard on writing, Joey often loses his train of thought. Joey sometimes brainstorms on the computer. He has used Inspiration to graphically organize his thoughts. He takes this graphic organizer and writes it into rough draft form. From there he uses his Alpha Smart Pro to type a final draft. The Alpha Smart Pro he uses was purchased by the school but Joey can take it home when he needs to complete assignments.

At the beginning of the year, Joey sat down with his resource teacher to help her read the manual and learn how to use the machine. At this point, he is an expert operator. He explains to other teachers and students how it works and how it helps him.

The Alpha Smart Pro has slightly enlarged keys so his fingers can find and hit them with accuracy. The Alpha Smart Pro looks something like a laptop computer. When Joey is ready to print a piece of work, he takes the Alpha Smart Pro to a teacher so he or she can hook it up to the classroom computer.

There are many benefits for Joey using the Alpha Smart Pro. He is able to complete assignments more quickly. His attitude toward writing has improved since his introduction to the machine. He gets less frustrated with simple tasks. His work is legible and easier to evaluate, and he is successfully learning how to use assistive technology. Despite the benefits, there are drawbacks as well. It is always a little difficult to be a child who is different. The Alpha Smart Pro causes Joey to stand out, as he is the only one typing while the other students are writing.

Overall, I think the Alpha Smart Pro is beneficial for Joey. His attitude toward writing has improved since his introduction to the machine. Joey is an excellent student and I enjoy working with him very much. I am sure his future will be rewarding as he successfully makes his way through the secondary school years.

SPEECH/LANGUAGE/COMMUNICATION DISORDERS

Susan Tucker-Kelley describes the tools she uses with her caseload of students with language development/communication disorders (2000):

Teach Me to Talk by SoftTouch benefits the student who is at the beginning stages of language development. The program utilizes over 150 Mayer-Johnson photographs of real objects. There are four activities in this program: Teach Me to Talk, Switch-On-Picts, Puzzle Play and Story Time. Clicking a button will display teaching hints for each activity.

The Teach Me to Talk activity is for students who are learning to match pictures to their spoken word names. Students see a photograph and hear the name of the photograph. A display of 6, 9 or 15 photographs may be selected. The photograph moves and morphs into a line drawing of the photo. A musical interlude plays in the background. The teacher has the option of turning off the music, movement or morphing features. The teacher may also deselect the symbol (line drawing) feature. The teacher can choose from particular categories of pictures to teach: five thematic categories (e.g., food, animals); three bilabial categories (p, b, m); and four general categories (encompasses a variety of picture types).

The Switch-On-Picts activity gives the student switch practice. A photograph appears on the screen with a picture of a switch in the bottom right corner. The photograph is named once and then the switch picture flashes repeatedly. If the teacher selects the verbal prompt option, the computer will say, "Press the switch." Once the switch (or mouse) is pressed the next picture appears. The teacher has the option to include music and/or movement with the photographs.

The Puzzle Play activity features 100 photographs from which to select. The teacher can choose 2, 3, 4, 8, or 16 puzzle pieces and has the option of selecting one of four different methods of completing the puzzle. For example, when the automatic manner is selected, the student selects a puzzle piece and the piece floats to the correct spot in the puzzle. When the puzzle is complete the name of the picture is spoken. The Story Time activity puts the training words into a short sentence structure using four-line English rhymes. Each line is highlighted as it is spoken. The teacher can choose rhymes by category or can select rhymes to play in sequence. A sample rhyme from the animal category goes like this:

> A dog will always bark,
> And a cow will say moo,
> And a pig likes to say oink,
> And a chicken goes cock-a-doodle-doo.

The use of real-life photographs helps students make the connection between a photograph and the concrete object the photograph represents. Both photographs and line drawings can be used in the Teach Me to Talk activity. This combination helps students make the visual transition from concrete to abstract pictures. The program is easily customized, and the music, movement and morphing features can be turned off for students who are easily distracted.

TalkTime with Tucker by Laureate Learning Systems is designed to help students increase their vocalizations. Wearing a headset microphone, a student can make Tucker move and respond by speaking into the mike. The program covers a range of communication processes and accepts a broad range of verbal input. It can be used sequentially from simple sounds or words to increased volume to increased sentence length to communicative exchanges. Five activities make up this program: On Stage, On the Farm, A Walk in the Woods, Fantasyland and Let's Talk. The student or teacher can select any of these activities in any order from the activity menu.

The On Stage activity features circus animals in the Amazing Animal Show. A student producing any sound can make an animal perform a trick. For example, Harry the Hippo directs, "Talk to me and I'll dance." After a response from the student Harry dances and then says, "Talk more and I'll jump." Harry's final trick is performed after the student responds to, "Say something else and I'll kick."

The On the Farm activity presents a variety of farm animals that encourage the student to speak. For example, a donkey states, "Donkeys say hee-haw. Talk to me and I'll show you how I kick."

The activity A Walk in the Woods encourages students to increase the length of their verbalizations. For instance, a mother bird directs, "Talk and make sounds and see how the eggs change. The longer you talk the more you'll see happen." As the student talks, eggs in a nest begin to crack open and baby birds emerge.

Tucker is a wizard who encounters fictional characters in the Fantasyland activity. Students adjust the volumes of their voices to make Tucker fly higher on his way to a castle. The characters Tucker encounters recite poems that encourage speech. For example, the knight recites, "I'm the knight who guards the magic door. Say the magic word and I will show you more."

The Let's Talk activity gives the student the opportunity to participate in a conversation. The student talks for Tucker who is being interviewed by Casey the Chameleon. Casey, who hosts his own talk show, asks Tucker a variety of open-ended questions.

Tiger's Tale, also by Laureate Learning Systems, is a tool that assists students with disfluencies, articulation errors and voice disorders. Using a microphone headset, students record and play back their own voices in order to talk for Tiger who has lost his voice. Tiger's animal friends ask questions to help the students formulate words to say. For example, Cookie the Cockatoo asks, "What would you say if you got hit in the head with a coconut?" Cookie also says, "Help Tiger stop the taxi" while the taxi is banging back and forth between two trees.

Students can select a story with 5, 10, or 14 scenes in it. With each animated scene presented, students have up to ten seconds to record a response for Tiger. Students then click the play-and-save button to hear their recording so that they can make changes if they wish. This button also saves the latest recording for inclusion in a movie drama. In the final scene students have to click on various objects to find the object that hides Tiger's voice. Once Tiger's voice is found, students view the "home movie" that features their voices as Tiger. Using the play-and-save button improves students' verbal productions. When they play back their voices they receive auditory feedback and can make revisions by saying sounds more clearly, saying sentences more fluently, and/or raising the volume of their voices."

STUDENT ACTIVITIES

1. Select a student to observe in at least three different settings (home, school, playground, or extracurricular). In at least one of the settings, observe the student using a computer to enhance some aspect of his or her life. Write a case study using the cases in this chapter as a model.

2. Make a list of the assistive devices and software listed in the case studies above. Identify the purpose of each device and the software and how it benefits the student.

3. For each of the students whom you serve, list the assistive device(s) and software they are currently using that are beneficial. List assistive devices and software that might be useful but are not currently available (what sort of advocacy might be required to insure access?).

REFERENCES

Anderson, K. (2001). Case study of Kevin. An unpublished manuscript for SPED 346C, California State University, Chico.

Bott, C. (1998). Augcomm system provides a voice for a young child with autism. *Tech-NJ, 10*(1),

Kelly, R. (2000). Technology for individuals who are deaf, hard of hearing, blind, and partially sighted. In J. Lindsey (Ed.), *Technology and exceptional individuals* (3rd ed., pp. 353–374). Austin, TX: Pro-Ed.

Langone, J. (2000). Technology for individuals with severe and physical disabilities. In J. Lindsey (Ed.), *Technology and exceptional individuals* (3rd ed., pp. 327–351). Austin, TX: Pro-Ed,

Lupo, T. (1997). Technology's role in the education of a blind student. *Tech-NJ, 8*(2),

Mullin, T. (2001). Case study of Danny. An unpublished manuscript for SPED 346C, California State University, Chico.

Okolo, C. (2000). Technology for individuals with mild disabilities. In J. Lindsey (Ed.), *Technology and exceptional individuals* (3rd ed., pp. 243–301). Austin, TX: Pro-Ed.

Smith, J. (2001). Case study of Joey. An unpublished manuscript for SPED 346C, California State University, Chico.

Storey, A. (2001). Case study of John. An unpublished manuscript for SPED 346C, California State University, Chico.

Tucker-Kelley, S. (2000). Can we talk? Software for language development. *Tech-NJ, 11*(1),

Vazquez, P. (2001). Case study of Alice. An unpublished manuscript for SPED 346C, California State University, Chico.

Wehmeyer, M. (1999). Assistive technology and students with mental retardation: Utilization and barriers. *Journal of Special Education Technology, 14*(1), 48–58.

Zhang, Y. (2000). Technology and the writing skills of students with learning disabilities. *Journal of Research on Computing in Education, 32*(4), 467–479.

■ ■ ■ ■ ■ ▬▬▬▬▬▬▬▬▬▬▬▬▬▬▬▬▬▬▬▬▬▬▬▬▬▬▬▬▬▬▬

CHAPTER SEVEN

TECHNOLOGY TRANSITIONS THROUGH THE LIFE CYCLE

Just sitting in a chair not talking
Just sitting in a chair not walking
Just sitting in a chair not using your board.
One day you would throw them away
Or you ain't no friend of mine.
When I can walk and talk and sit.
Just play the game and you can win.
I will fight until I am 50009008
And in my grave.
I can do some thing
But I want to do more.
Just sitting in a chair not having fun.
Just sitting in a chair not playing.
Just sitting in a chair not moving.
Maybe one day it will come true.
Just sitting in a chair watching your friends.
I hope it comes true.

Jason was ten years old when he wrote that poem (Burcat, 1995); at 16, technology has changed his life substantially. He uses a Liberator for augmentative communication, a power wheelchair, finds information using an encyclopedia on his CD-ROM and the Internet, and loves to play computer games with friends. He has a specially equipped game system. All aspects of his life are enhanced by access to technology.

Academic development and productivity are significant areas in which technology can play a major role. However, technology can also play a major role in offering options for recreation and leisure, art and music, and social and career development. This chapter focuses on how technology can offer enriching options beyond school.

CHAPTER GOALS

By the end of this chapter, you will have:

1. explored ways in which technology can improve the quality of life for the students you serve in situations outside of school;

2. learned how to select technology options for developing functional and life skills specific to the students you serve;

3. learned how to ensure that all aspects of a student's life are addressed by the educational program and supported by technology when appropriate.

INFANTS AND TODDLERS AND THE EARLY CHILDHOOD YEARS: AT HOME AND AT SCHOOL

What is the best way to select technology interventions for very young children? Regardless of any special needs, babies and very young children need a wide variety of opportunities to explore, control their environment, and communicate with caregivers. Most importantly, children need to play!

Toys

Adapted toys, appropriate for any baby, can be made inexpensively at home or school using resources purchased from companies specializing in adapted toys, or checked out from a lending library established specifically for that purpose such as CompuPlay projects set up by the National Lekotek Center, Alliance for Technology Access centers (see list in Appendix B), or federally funded Parent Information Centers. If the child has a physical disability, a good source of ideas for adapted toys may be the occupational or physical therapist in your child's school or preschool program.

Battery-operated toys, for example, can be operated by manipulating a switch, which gives the child control of the activity. Infants as young as three months old have used a combination of toys and computers to discover relationships between what they do and their environment. These activities can also stimulate motor development when the toys and switches are positioned in certain ways. Because these toys and computers are appealing to babies with a wide variety of abilities, these tools are perfect for an inclusive environment in the home, in a play group, or in an educational setting. After getting used to operating switch-operated toys, a child can make an easier transition to operating a computer.

Communication Aids

Communication aids and augmentative communication devices may represent, to the educator, an opportunity for a very young child to become more independent with communication. For a parent, however, the decision to use adaptive devices for communication may be more complex. The hope or dream of a child learning to talk or to sign may be threatened by the proposed tool. One mother, a former speech therapist, described it this way: "It was just, to me, going to something like that is really a sad thing, kind of. I mean, it's like…I've always been enthused about using signing…I started with Dawn signing right away, and I just remembered when she was just an infant, how she picked up 'shoe' and, you know, being excited about that. I didn't anticipate that it wouldn't go on from there, that we would not get more speech, and then going to this kind of system is kind of like the

FIGURE 7.1

end of a long…I mean, I want something to work for her and I'm glad about the things they have for that, but it's not, you know.…" (Todis, 1996, p. 51).

Professionals must take great care to proceed with compassion and understanding and to help parents balance the desire for "normalized" goals for their child with the benefits of learning to use a device early to achieve more independence and progress, perhaps, in other arenas. They must also take care not to "oversell" the benefits of the device, which may or may not result in the miraculous gains a parent dreams of. As one parent said: "The ACC device I thought would be the answer to all my prayers, and it is presented like that. I don't know if it is presented that way on purpose. I don't think it is meant to hurt anybody when people do present it that way, they are just excited. That is great. I want people to keep up the enthusiasm. But tell [parents] it is not an answer to every problem and everything…It won't always fit into every little nook and cranny of everybody's life" (Todis, 1996, p. 51). Finally, professionals must do their best to encourage and support parents in their quest for tools and devices that may be successful for their child. One parent summed it up this way: "What's very frustrating in schools here is that we invest money into using the [ACC device] and they [school staff] want her to use her body [eye gaze and facial expression]. I want somebody [in the public school] that works with me that really has interest [in ACC]…I'm not saying they are not out there but in the basic school I haven't stumbled into it…It is just really interesting when all these people say 'Uh, well, she is not going to do this [use her ACC device appropriately].' Well, if I could predict the future like that I could probably make a lot of money doing it. I don't see how people can be so negative about it (Todis, 1996, p. 51)."

Computers

Jonathan (age 3) has used a computer since he was six months old. He began with the Muppet Learning Keys, cackling with delight when pressing a key activated a Sesame Street character. At about eighteen months, he moved on to the Macintosh regular keyboard and developed very precise motor control of the mouse, pointing and selecting what he wanted from programs such as Bailey's Book House and Thinkin' Things with the greatest of care. Now he treats the computer as a tool and a companion, experimenting with speech output, telling stories to Mom, who types them in, and then selecting the "Read Aloud" button to hear his stories read over and over again—far more often than even patient Mom could bear to do it. When friends come to visit, he brings them straight up to the computer, where he proudly offers to show them his skills and to let them have a turn making a picture or playing a game. In this way, he participates as an equal with a wide age and ability range of people—just as he will have to be prepared to do in real life!

Computers can provide access to a wide variety of play activities that are an essential part of early child development. Selecting appropriate software is the key; keeping in mind what is developmentally appropriate and what is engaging and appealing to each child is crucial.

Among the goals of early learning software are (Dell & Newton, 1998):

- visual attention and visual tracking;
- cause and effect;
- receptive language (i.e., understanding words and pictures);
- pre-academics, or "basic concepts," such as shapes, colors, sizes, and patterns;
- early reading and writing skills such as letter recognition, consonant and vowel sounds, simple sight words, and simple sentence structure;
- early critical thinking skills such as memory and simple problem solving;
- emergent literacy (i.e., developing an interest in words and reading);
- play and exploration.

Dell and Newton (1998) also offer suggestions about ways of assessing the types of software that might be appropriate. Table 7.1 summarizes questions to ask and some examples of software that might be selected in particular situations.

Guidelines for successfully incorporating technology at very early ages include the following:

- Assume that there are no prerequisites for language acquisition and that every child has the capacity to learn.
- Use the child's own reality and meaning system to construct activities, not isolated tasks constructed in a hierarchy of prerequisites (cause and effect, switch use, picture recognition, toy recognition, visual scanning, etc.) on the computer.
- Make sure the child's positioning needs are assessed and addressed so that the appropriate type of switch, keyboard, or slantboard can be used.
- Use the computer to promote social skills and increase interaction with peers or caregivers.

Art

At every stage in life, art can provide a wonderful medium for self-expression, demonstrating learning, and communicating, and just plain fun! An example of a cooperatively structured lesson plan appropriate for the early learning years was developed by Wendy Brooks (Figure 7.2).

TABLE 7.1 Selecting Software for Young Children

QUESTION TO ASK	GOAL FOR THE CHILD	SPECIFIC SOFTWARE
What do I want the computer experience to do for the child?	Have fun playing and exploring	Kid Pix
	Develop child's interest in words and reading	Kaleidoscope
		Living Books, Magic Tales, Disney Animated Storybooks
	Reinforce school skills such as shapes, colors, early reading or math skills	Millie's Math House, Bailey's Book House, A to Zap!
What features does the child need?	Visual impairment and nonreaders	Speech output
	Visual perception problems	Consistent, uncluttered display
	Motor difficulties, stress in timed situations	Self-paced
	Opportunities to do things independently	Active learning—"explore"and and "answer" modes
		Appropriate feedback—child can distinguish right and wrong answers and is not rewarded by animations and sound effects for incorrect answers
Can the program be customized to fit the child's needs?	All	Control of difficulty level (such as easy, medium, or difficult) or automatic branching as child gets correct or incorrect answers
		Program remembers where child left off
		Control how long the program will wait for an answer
		Specify the skills desired
	English language learner	Mouse click changes from English to Spanish
	Visual impairment	Change size and image of the cursor
What is the child interested in?	All	Software with choices:
		Interactive storybooks
		Reader Rabbit Toddler for children who like to sing
		Franklin's Activity Center for children who love animals
	Physical disability	Blocks in Motion
Is the program easy to use?	All	Easy-to-follow instructions
		Each program in a series uses the same format/structure
How will the child access the program?	Physical disabilities	Alternative access devices such as trackballs, touchscreens, expanded keyboards

Adapted from Dell and Newton, *Exceptional Parent* magazine by special permission: 1998, Psy-Ed Corp. All rights reserved.

FIGURE 7.2 KidPix Lesson Plan

Grade Level: K–2

Subject: Color recognition

Length: 30 minutes maximum per trial

The Lesson: Students will use Kid Pix software to illustrate *Rolie Polie Olie, Little Spot of Color* by William Joyce. They will use the program to make the same color of 'spots and dots' like Olie does and they will need to 'clean' the 'spots and dots' like Olie does in the book.

Group size: 3 students

Group Assignment: Groups will be selected with one high functioning, one medium functioning, and one low functioning student. At least one will know colors fairly consistently.

Materials Needed: Kid Pix, "Little Spot of Color" by William Joyce

Assigning Tasks: Each group member will have a turn to make a 'spot' or 'dot' of color using the mouse or touch screen. The whole group will be involved in naming the colors.

The Task: "Little Spot of Color" will be read for about the 20+ time. The students are encouraged to name the colors before the teacher gives them any kind of verbal or sign language clue. This will give the teacher the information for structuring the groups. Once the book is read and the teacher has divided the students into groups, the first group will begin the task. Because some of the students are at the matching color stage, the book can be used as a reference for those students only. The students who are higher functioning will be required to remember, name, and select the correct color. The group will be expected to create a wall just like Olie did in the book, consisting of all the colors. There should be more than five 'spots and dots' of each color (it looks splatter painted). There will be no real structure to the finished product. The only requirement is that all the colors are represented on the 'wall.' When the 'wall' is completed and checked, the group will print out their creation. Then the students will take turns 'cleaning' the 'spots and dots,' just as Olie cleaned the 'spots and dots,' using the eraser mechanism on the program with the mouse or touch screen.

Positive Interdependence: Each member of the group will contribute to naming the colors, creating the 'wall' and 'cleaning' the 'wall.'

Individual Accountability: Every member of the group will have to name or match one color and begin to make the 'spots and dots' of that color.

Criterion for Success: The group will have a printout of their project and a 'cleaned' screen.

Specific Behaviors Expected: Turn taking, sharing knowledge, task completion, patience for those who are not as advanced.

Evidence of Expected Behaviors: No one is taking over all of the mouse or touch screen process; no raised voices; each member gets to use the mouse/touch screen in a precise order.

Plans for Processing: Printouts will be hung around the room so they can be utilized at any time by a student. The book will continue to be read everyday at circle time and each student's growth will be measured by a paraprofessional.

One commentator has said of the latest version of Kid Pix: "Kid Pix Deluxe 3 is a masterpiece of art creativity software. Kid Pix Deluxe 3 allows children to create art at their computers, save it, send it to friends and family over the Internet, and even place it into a streaming video slide show" (Gudmundsen, 2001). Easy to use, powerful in the variety of means for creating and sharing art, Kid Pix Deluxe 3 is a wonderful addition to a school or family software collection.

ELEMENTARY SCHOOL: RECREATIONAL ACTIVITIES

Music

Music is an inclusive, engaging activity for all ages and abilities. At a simple level, students can play pre-made songs, revise them and record the changes, write songs, or learn to read music and understand rhythm. Rock Rap 'n Roll offers students a choice of musical styles from which to select. Students can save prerecorded sequences in their preferred order, and record themselves singing or playing instruments with background accompaniment (McCord, 2001). This easy-to-use program provides success quickly and the results sound terrific! The program is controlled by keyboard, mouse, or adaptive mouse devices for students with physical disabilities.

Making Music software gives students a chance to compose their own music, using graphic notation that is "painted" onto the screen. Students can visually paint in high or low pitches and hear high or low sounds. Students can feel, see, and hear pitch at the same time, which optimizes a multisensory approach to music learning.

Children who are interested in music fundamentals will enjoy Music Ace and Music Ace 2, which include games to teach music notation. The music is notated in colored faces that smile when they sound. The program speaks all text and rewards students for correct answers. Using the Doodle Pad, students can create their own music by placing notes and durations on the staff. The music can be recorded for playback. Students can also select prerecorded songs from a jukebox and edit them.

Two programs are especially useful for students with visual impairments: Finale and Goodfeel. Notes can be enlarged on the screen and in printouts. With a MIDI keyboard, students can play pieces that are converted to musical notation. Goodfeel enables budding composers to write their own music and print it in Braille. This program also speaks all text.

For children with cognitive disabilities, Children's Songbook offers prerecorded songs from various countries. The notation is highlighted while playing and provides background "movies" that help students remember what the song is about. Song lyrics appear in English as well as in the original language.

Superswitchensemble works with Overlay Maker for the IntelliKeys adaptive keyboard so that students can use switches to use a MIDI keyboard. More than 100 songs are included in the program. This program is useful for children with physical and/or cognitive disabilities.

In Brooklyn's Public School 36K, students work at stations equipped with MIDI keyboards and percussion pads. As students play, computer software translates their musi-

TABLE 7.2   Music Software Web Sites

SOFTWARE TITLE	WEB SITE ADDRESS
Children's Songbook	*www.learntech.com/cdrom*
Goodfeel	*www.dancingdots.com*
Finale 2001	*www.codamusic.com*
Music Ace and Music Ace 2	*www.harmonicvision.com*
Rock Rap 'n Roll	*www.scottforesman.com*

cal efforts into notation. Miriam Klein, principal, points out: "They don't have to know how to read or write regular music, but in creating the music, they learn about musical notation." She finds that the music software helps students with fractions, with science (sound waves and principles of hearing), and other subjects as well, not to mention social skills, as students work together on their musical pieces and give feedback to each other. The learning takes many different directions.

Table 7.2 provides Web sites for the music software described above.

Games

Games can be designed for review of academic content, for development of problem-solving and strategy skills, or purely for fun. The Journey of the Zoombinis, for example, helps students think about attributes and use these skills to make decisions about the best strategy to guide the Zoombinis on their Incredible Journey, a program that captures the complete attention of the players! The Sims series gives children a chance to make design decisions (SimSkiResort, SimThemePark) or to manipulate the lives of a "cyber" family as they go about their daily activities.

Games can stimulate children's curiosity about their neighborhood or the world, using mapmaking software or playing detective games (Where in the World is Carmen Sandiego? series). They can use their design skills to make their own games and test them out with other children or to make games for younger students.

ADOLESCENCE

Pressures to prepare for making difficult choices begin to build in the adolescent years. These may be personal choices involving sex, drugs, truancy, and the like, or they may be related to choosing a career or deciding whether to apply for college or continued training in a particular field.

The computer can be used in a number of ways to help teens acquire information they need to make these decisions, look at the consequences of decisions in a simulated environment, and practice skills they will need once they are out of school and on their own.

Table 7.3 provides a sample of software programs that teachers have used with success in working with adolescents to develop appropriate social skills (Walker & Williamson, 1995).

TABLE 7.3 Social Skills and Commercial Software

SOFTWARE PROGRAM	SOCIAL SKILLS
Blueprint for Decision Making	Decision making and problem solving in peer and authority figure relationships, and dealing with group pressure
Choices, Choices	Decision making, problem solving, cause–effect, dealing with group pressure, expressing feelings, and listening skills in peer relationships
Taking Responsibility	Honesty, decision making, and responsibility in peer and authority figure relationships
On the Playground	Initiating and mainataining relationship skills, decision making in peer relationships
Following Directions: Life Skills Series Set 1	Following directions and listening
Interviewing: Life Skills Series Set 1	Receptive and expressive verbal and nonverbal communication skills, and understanding the feelings of others
On the Job: Life Skills Series Set 1	Asking a question, asking for help, giving and following instructions
The Mirror Inside Us: Life Skills Series Set 1	Knowing and expressing feelings, dealing with anger and criticism, and reward

FROM SCHOOL TO WORK

The computer skills students have built throughout their years in school can have major impacts on several areas in their adult lives, such as job/vocational options, personal/professional productivity, recreational activities, and access to information and resources. Within vocational training programs and within educational training programs, students with special needs can benefit from specific activities to prepare them for life after school.

One way that teachers prepare their students for life after school is through simulations of real-life situations using technology. Leslie Cramer, a special education teacher, has designed a cooperative computer lesson on budgeting using a spreadsheet, included below in Figure 7.3.

Another example of using technology to learn real-life skills is special education teacher Vanessa Staudacher's lesson on riding the bus, Figure 7.4.

Job/Vocational Options

Not everyone will want to become a computer scientist, engineer, or programmer, but almost everyone who has successful skills with computers will be able to find a job. Data entry, reservationist, cashier, clerical, graphic arts, mechanics—all these fields require computer skills. Students who have developed these skills, whose needs for access have been evaluated and updated as new and improved devices have been implemented, will have advantages over other job applicants. Tables 7.4 and 7.5 provide an overview of software helpful in developing functional life skills and in career/vocational development.

FIGURE 7.3   Spreadsheet Budgeting Activity

Students are paired together as married couples/roommates. Given two scenarios, each pair of students will create two monthly budgets using spreadsheets. In each scenario students will be given the monthly incomes of each member of the household along with the couple's daily expenditures for one month. Students will transfer these expenditures from their scenario sheet and place each of them into the appropriate budgeting category on their spreadsheets. Students will then have the computer tally the monthly expenditures. Following a class discussion concerning each pair's findings, each team will complete a worksheet for each scenario that will serve to summarize those findings. Each student will also write a reflection paper in which he or she will discuss certain questions related to his or her experience with the budgeting activity.

Subject Areas: problem solving, life skills, math, cooperative learning skills, spreadsheet skill development.

Grade Level: 6th–12th

1. *Objectives:*
   A. Students will use their problem-solving skills to help them track and organize budgets from two scenarios.
   B. Students will learn how to organize data using spreadsheets.
   C. Students will display an understanding about the cost of living in our society today.
   D. Students will work cooperatively with another student in order to complete this assignment.
2. *Materials Needed:* Spreadsheet software, scenario guide, spreadsheet instruction sheet
3. *Time Required:* 3.5–4 hours per team over a two-week period
4. *Procedures:*
   A. Preparation:
      1. Review spreadsheet instructional guide as I discuss how to use spreadsheets with the class.
      2. Practice transferring data into the made-up spreadsheet on the computer using the spreadsheet instruction guide for assistance.
      3. Pair students into teams.
   B. Set:
      1. Ask students how much they think it would cost them to live on their own for a month. Students will be given 20 minutes to brainstorm and write down all of the monthly expenses they think they will incur.
      2. When you set out to live on your own, one skill that you must have is the knowledge of how to budget your money adequately. Without this knowledge, you may find yourself overspending and getting yourself into debt. Throughout the next two weeks I will show you how to budget your money easily using spreadsheets.
   C. Input:
      1. With your partner, enter the following data (found on your scenario guide), in order, onto your spreadsheet template.
      2. Enter the monthly paycheck amounts for partner #1 and partner #2 in the labeled sections on your spreadsheet.

FIGURE 7.3   Continued

3. Enter the fixed monthly expense amounts into their labeled categories: monthly rent, utilities, car payment, and car insurance payment.
4. Enter the roommates/couples daily expenses, which should be recorded along with the date of purchase, in the appropriate dated cell on your spreadsheet.
5. After entering your daily expenses in the dated calendar on your spreadsheet, enter each daily expense in its appropriate category on the left-hand side of your spreadsheet. Example: The cost of two movie tickets would be entered in the Entertainment category.
6. The computer will automatically tally your expenses.
D. Independent Practice:
1. On completion of their spreadsheet budget, teams will be given a worksheet that will summarize their findings to complete together. The following questions will be included:
2. What was the combined income of the partners in your scenario?
3. How much did they spend on utilities every month? Car payments? Car insurance? Rent? Food? Entertainment? Clothing? Gasoline for the car? What about expenses that didn't fit into any of these categories? What was the total of the couple's monthly expenditures? Did the couple go over their monthly budget? Why? Do you feel that the couple overspent in certain areas? Which ones? Why do you feel this way?
4. Each student will write a reflection paper that will summarize his or her budget scenario findings and emphasize his or her personal opinions and feelings about the project. I will also have the students explain how knowing how to use spreadsheets can be valuable in helping them organize and keep track of data in their daily lives.
E. Closure:
Following completion of the Spreadsheet Budget Findings Worksheet and the student reflection papers, we will have a whole class discussion concerning each team's findings and personal thoughts about budgeting.

FIGURE 7.4   When Does the Bus Get There?

Topic: Transportation

Focus: Study Skills, Self-Help Skills

Goal: The student will be able to answer all of the questions on the activity sheet by using the Internet, a chart, and a time table.

ACTIVITY SHEET
Directions:

- Study the bus schedule for the Chester to Quincy route. You can find and print that schedule on the Internet at: *http://www.aworkforce.org/ptransit/ctoq.htm*
- You will also need to study the fares at: *http://www.aworkforce.org/ptransit/fares.htm*

(continued)

FIGURE 7.4 Continued

- Use the schedule and fare page to answer the questions below.

1. At what time in the morning does the first bus leave Holiday Market? _____

2. What time does that bus arrive at Safeway? _____
3. What time does the last bus arrive at Safeway? _____
4. How many trips does the bus make a day? _____
5. What time does the second bus reach Canyon Dam? _____
6. Valerie works at the Evergreen Market. She gets on the bus at Sierra Meadows Apartments. She has to be at work by 4:30 P.M. What time should she be at the bus stop? _____
7. According to the fare information sheet, how much would Valerie have to pay? _____

8. Edgar wants to make it to the post office by 3:00 P.M. in order to get there before it closes. When is the latest pickup from his stop at Marie and Lorraine that he can take? _____
9. If Valerie worked everyday at the Evergreen Market, and took the bus, should she buy the monthly pass or not? _____ Why? _____

TABLE 7.4 Functional Skills Software

SOFTWARE TITLE	PRODUCER
Edmark Functional Word Series: Signs Around You, 1 and 2	Edmark
Touch Money	Edmark
A Day in the Life…Instruction	Curriculum Associates

TABLE 7.5 Career/Vocational Development Software

SOFTWARE TITLE	PRODUCER
Blueprint for Decision Making	Lawrence Productions
Career Surveys	Conover Company
Functional Skills Screening Inventory	Functional Assessment and Training Consultants
Job Readiness	Lawrence Productions
Job Attitudes	Lawrence Productions
Job Search and Local Job Bank	Conover Company
Job Success Series	Lawrence Productions
On the Job Series: Career Interests, Communication Skills, Competency-Based Mathematics I & II, Problem-Solving	Conover Company
Jobs in Today's World	Lawrence Productions

Vocational Training

With the advent of high-stakes testing as a prerequisite to a high school diploma, many parents and schools are asking, "What will happen to our children?" Many high school special education and general education programs are rethinking their curriculum and services to better prepare students in special education for the tests; other high schools are looking at a wider array of vocational training options for students who may never pass the high school exit exam.

In New York, for example, some high schools are explicitly linking secondary vocational curricula to the knowledge and skills that employers demand. In the Greenburgh-North Castle district, for example, students can participate in the American Airlines Travel Academy, earning community college credits and a real-world certification (Donlevy, 1999). The curriculum consists of more than 300 hours of instruction in the reservations system and covers world geography, ticketing, customer service, and communication skills. Students with special needs are able to complete this demanding curriculum in three specially designed segments rather than the intensive original program design. A second program in the district features a certificate in computer-aided design, recognized by Microsoft. A third element of the vocational preparation at Greenburgh-North Castle includes explicit articulation with community colleges, so that students can begin earning community college credits while still in high school.

The design and vision of these programs assumes that students will already have had extensive experience and skills in using computers as they move through the schools. In far too many schools, students in special education do not have equitable access to computer resources. Teachers, parents, and service providers will need to be more effective advocates for these students if the possibilities described above are to become reality.

Environmental Control

Many people are accustomed to various remote control or computerized devices in their homes, such as those used for televisions, VCRs, microwave ovens, thermostats, and the like. Whether these devices offer merely convenience or a means of providing environmental control, these options present people with the opportunity for normalized, independent

FIGURE 7.5   A student can operate a blender and participate in independent living experiences.

living with reduced dependence on others for comfort and even survival. With current technology, the computer can be used to control a security system, turn lights on and off, operate kitchen appliances, and even have a robot deliver dinner.

Access to Information and Resources

Access to the Internet (see Chapter 8), provides a means for getting and sending needed information instantly, without having to leave one's home. Paying bills, shopping for groceries (and virtually anything else), communicating with friends and colleagues, working out of one's home—E-mail enables those with a variety of needs and abilities to communicate without the interference or stigma of wheelchairs, sign language, Braille, and so forth. Electronic equality for all!

LONG-RANGE PLANNING FOR TECHNOLOGY THROUGH THE LIFE CYCLE

One purpose of this chapter has been to illustrate several principles about incorporating technology into one's life:

1. There is no minimum age.
2. There is no maximum age.
3. Computer skills are not developmental, and prerequisites should not apply.
4. Computer skills are infinitely expandable to new situations, software, and hardware.
5. Computer skills benefit people of varying levels of abilities, interests, and ages, and can be adapted to virtually any situation.

In making decisions about using technology, imagine the child at a later stage of development, recognizing, of course, that technology will change and improve all along the way.

STUDENT ACTIVITIES

1. Interview a student who actively uses technology as a part of life outside of school. What activities does the student do? What benefits does technology offer? What additional ideas do you have for expanding opportunities for the student using technology (e.g., recreation, career/vocational, independence)?

2. Select a student in your program (or your own child). Imagine that student five years in the future. In what kinds of technology activities do you see the student involved? In what ways will his or her technology needs be different? In what ways will technology support increased academic success, leisure and recreation, independence, and vocational/career choices?

3. Review the programs of your students and assess the role of technology. Has assistive technology been considered? Is it being used wisely? Are there assistive devices that would enhance the students' productivity that are not being used?

REFERENCES

Brooks, W. (2001). Cooperative lesson plan for early learners. Unpublished paper for California State University Chico SPED 346C.

Burcat, B. (1995). Technology provides independence. *TECH-NJ, 6*(1), 4–5.

Cramer, L. (2001). Spreadsheet lesson plan. Unpublished paper for California State University Chico SPED 346C.

Dell, A., & Newton, D. (1998). Software for PLAY and ACTIVE Early Learning. *The Exceptional Parent, 28*(11), 39–43.

Donleavy, J. (1999). Reaching higher standards: Special education, real-world certifications in technology and the community college connection. *International Journal of Instructional Media, 26*(3), 241–248.

Gudmundsen, J. (2001, April 12). These programs give children virtual canvases for creativity. *San Jose Mercury News,* (Technology Section p. 1).

McCord, K. (2001). Music software for special needs. *Music Educators Journal, 87*(4), 30–5, 64.

Staudacher, V. (2001). Lesson plan on transportation. Unpublished paper for SPED 346C, California State University, Chico.

Todis, B. (1996). Tools for the Task? Perspectives on Assistive Technology in Educational Settings. *Journal of Special Education Technology, 13,* 49–61.

Walker, D., & Williamson, R. (1995). Computers and adolescents with emotional/behavioral disorders: Developing social skills and social competency. *Closing the Gap, 14*(3), 24–27.

CHAPTER EIGHT

EMPOWERING TEACHERS, STUDENTS, AND FAMILIES WITH THE INTERNET

The Internet as a transformational tool for empowerment is evident in almost every aspect of life for children and adults, in and outside of schools. Reading and writing E-mails, shopping, planning travel, finding information, managing information; no aspect of life is untouched! In this chapter, we examine the ways teachers, students, and their families can use the Internet to expand their access to learning, resources, materials, and ideas. One national study demonstrates that students with on-line access perform better than those without Internet access on measurements of information management, communication, and presentation of ideas (CAST, 2000).

CHAPTER GOALS

By the end of this chapter, you will have explored:

1. the impact of the internet on teaching, learning, and communicating;
2. the benefits of Web-supported learning;
3. how to design Web-supported projects and learning activities, scaffolded and structured so that every student can be successful;
4. ideas and examples of project-based and Web-supported learning.

HOW THE INTERNET TRANSFORMS OUR THINKING ABOUT TEACHING AND LEARNING

Many teachers conceive of the Internet as an electronic encyclopedia for gathering information without fully realizing the transformative aspects of the Internet and its relationship to learning and teaching. Early research on the impact of student research using the Internet reveals the disappointing results of current classroom practices (Becker, 1998). The Internet does, certainly, put information at hand, but that is far from its most empowering characteristic. Now students must know how to evaluate the information they collect, how to make sense and interpret the information they have collected, and, most importantly, how to generate new ideas and formulate even more sophisticated questions as a result of their explorations (Mackenzie, 2000).

Tapscott (1999) summarizes eight fundamental shifts that must be acknowledged if teachers, students, and families are to fully utilize the empowering characteristics of the Internet:

1. From linear to nonlinear (hypermedia) learning and thinking: The traditional modes of learning have been linear: textbooks, videotapes, television shows, and so forth are all designed to be used with a particular sequence in mind. Access to information on the Internet, however, is much more interactive and nonlinear. Links enable learners to move from point to point of their own choosing, rather than in a sequence determined by someone else.

2. From instruction to construction and discovery: The Internet provides multiple options for learning about a concept, gathering examples, and sharing ideas. A much more hands-on, actively engaging type of learning occurs when students are given the tools to discover for themselves ideas and principles, rather than having the teacher dole them out.

3. From teacher-centered to learner-centered: Once students experience the exhilaration of discovering, they can be in charge of their own learning and have access to an entire universe of information. Teachers and parents no longer can control or limit the scope of their child's imagination.

4. From concentrating on memorizing facts and information to learning how to navigate and how to learn: The focus in an Internet-oriented classroom's learning style moves toward responding to a question with "I know where to find that answer" and "I understand why that's important and how that is related to ___."

5. From school as a stage of life to lifelong learning: Students, families and service providers recognize the importance of learning at all stages of life, not just in school, and not just K–12.

6. From one-size-fits-all learning activities and assignments to a recognition of individuality: On the Internet, different interests, skills, and styles, which result in a variety of ways of taking in and expressing learning, are all equally appropriate, in Papert's words, "a flexibility that could allow every individual to find personal paths to learning. This will make it possible for the dream of every progressive educator to come true: In the learning environment of the future, every learner will be 'special'" (1996, p. 16).

7. From learning as something to be enduring to learning as something to be enjoyed: Flexibility in pacing, interaction, learning styles, modes of expression, and more are all possible using Web-supported learning. Rather than feeling threatened by a shift from old ways of thinking about learning, educators and parents have an opportunity to participate in a whole new way of thinking about teaching and learning that offers even more benefits to students who have not been successful in traditional classrooms.

8. From a teacher as transmitter of facts to the teacher as facilitator of learning: Teachers move toward more opportunities to authentically assess each student's skills, interests, and needs and provide a menu of options for mastering ideas, concepts, and skills.

BASIC INTERNET TERMINOLOGY

Here are some basic terms that students, teachers, and families use when describing various aspects of the Internet:

- HTML—(hypertext markup language)—the computer language in which Web pages are written; combines text and graphics;
- browser—software that translates HTML computer code into material that is viewed on Web pages (Forcier, 1999). Popular examples include: Netscape Navigator and Microsoft Internet Explorer;
- hypertext—text written in a form to use links to jump from topic to topic instead of text written only in linear sequential form. By clicking on the highlighted text, which is usually in a different color, the user jumps automatically to the Web site's home page;
- URL (Uniform Resource Locator)—the address of a Web site, such as *http://www.yahoo.com*;
- search engines—an index, directory, or catalog organized by subject area that can be accessed by search terms (Forcier, 1999), for example, *www.google.com, www.AltaVista.com,* and *www.Yahoo.com;*
- ISP (Internet Service Provider)—a service that enables subscribers (users pay a monthly fee for access) to connect to the Internet, for example, America On-Line, Compuserve, and Earthlink;
- ISDN (Integrated Service Digital Network) and DSL (digital service line)—high-speed internet connection, faster than modems on regular phone lines;
- chat rooms—a designated place for participants to "chat" on-line at the same time. It is different from a "bulletin board" or "discussion board" where participants can review each other's comments and post public responses without needing to be on-line at the same time;
- distribution lists—most Internet Service Providers offer an "address book" function that stores names and E-mail addresses, either individually or in groups. In this way, teachers can send messages to all parents or students in a class at the same time, for example. "Listservs" are similar to distribution lists, except that they are usually done by subscription, organized around a shared interest, and administered by a third party.

PROJECT-BASED AND WEB-SUPPORTED LEARNING

With the Internet, finding information and pasting it into documents is a trivial, superficial, and static exercise, harnessing little of a student's brainpower. Instead, teachers can use the Internet as an opportunity for students to think deeply about essential questions. Instead of the traditional topical approach (e.g., finding out about missions, states, countries, or historical events), students should begin with research questions that require problem solving, decision making, or the generation of new solutions or ideas. The research cycle suggested by Mackenzie (2000) includes the following steps:

1. Questioning: What are the questions beneath the topic to be researched?

2. Planning: What is the most efficient/effective way to gather reliable information? How will we keep track of the information that is generated from a search?

3. Gathering: How can we reduce the information to that which adds value to our search, rather than just volume?

4. Sorting/sifting: What, exactly, are we looking for? Which pieces of information do the best job of answering our research questions?

5. Synthesizing: How can we move the information around, like puzzle pieces, to formulate conclusions?

6. Evaluating: Do we have everything we need to respond to our questions, or should we keep looking?

7. Reporting: How can we present our information in ways that engage the audience, focusing deeply on the heart of the content, not on the glitz of the presentation?

One tool that many teachers use to introduce students to doing research on the Internet is the **Webquest.** A Webquest is a carefully structured and scaffolded investigation that contains some Internet sites that can help students initiate their search, questions and note-taking guides for help shaping their data analysis, and a rubric for evaluating the quality of what they've discovered. A matrix of excellent examples of Webquests in a variety of subject areas and grade levels is found at *http://edweb.sdsu.edu/webquest/matrix.html.* Figure 8.1 provides an example of how to engage in a Webquest.

For teachers new to the idea of designing their own Webquests, Burkhart and Kelly (1999) offer this step-by-step approach:

Step 1. Become comfortable with the Internet

Step 2. Select appropriate Web sites.

Step 3. Set a clear objective/outcome for what you expect the students to learn from this experience.

Step 4. Reflect on how the use of the technology/Internet will enhance the achievement of the outcome.

Step 5. Preview all Web sites carefully.

Step 6. Decide if this experience would be most effective as a large group presentation, accessed directly by students, or as a combination of both.

Step 7. Make a bookmark list of the site or sites you will be using in the lesson and save them as a bookmark file in the global shared folder.

Step 8. Prepare a graphic organizer, rubric, or set of directions for students.

Step 9. Prepare students for what they will be learning and what will be expected of them.

Step 10. Plan for how you will assess mastery of the objective.

FIGURE 8.1   **Example of a Webquest**

Out of Darkness

The Story of Louis Braille

A Webquest for 4th and 5th Grades (Language Arts, Science)

Designed by Maryanne Pineo

mpineo@hdo.net

Introduction | Task | Process | Evaluation | Conclusion |

INTRODUCTION

Louis Braille was blinded at the age of three. When he was 15, he developed an alphabet system for the visually impaired. Let's find out what it would be like to be blind and use Braille to read and write. At the conclusion of this webquest, design an invention that would make life easier and more inclusive for people with visual impairments.

THE TASK

To better understand the book, *Out of Darkness: The Story of Louis Braille* by Russell Freedman, you will:

- experience blindness;
- investigate uses of Braille for the visually impaired;
- demonstrate how people who are blind do everyday things;
- design an invention that would assist persons with visual impairments to participate in everyday life.

THE PROCESS

1. Before you read *Out of Darkness: The Story of Louis Braille* by Russell Freedman:
   a. Close your eyes tightly, get a piece of paper out of your binder, get out a pencil, write your name on the paper.
   b. Think about your experience of being without sight trying to do a typical school activity. In a class discussion, share your experience.
   c. Brainstorm and chart activities that a blind person:
      - could do as easily as a sighted person
      - could not do easily
      - could do with accommodations.
2. Read the book *Out of Darkness:The Story of Louis Braille* by Russell Freedman.
3. After reading the book find out more about how people who are blind do everyday things. You will demonstrate the following things to the class:
   a. how blind people pick out their clothes;
   b. how blind people identify money;
   c. how blind people cook.

   The National Federation of the Blind's Web site has links to a great deal of information for people who are visually impaired. Click on *questions kids ask about being blind* to find out how blind people do everyday things.

FIGURE 8.1   Continued

4. Go to *101 uses of Braille* to investigate how Braille is used by the visually impaired; make a list of at least ten uses. This link is an article on the many practical uses of Braille, and is one of many on the *National Federation of the Blind's* Web site.

5. Think about a situation in everyday life that would be difficult for a person with visual impairments. From what you have learned in the previous activities and about how Louis Braille invented the Braille alphabet, design an invention and describe your invention to the class. Make a model.

EVALUATION

You can earn up to 100 points on this webquest.

      0   **Minimal**
      5   **Adequate**
   10   **Good Job**
   15   **Exemplary**

Activity 1
Experience, reflect/share thoughts about being blind

    Closed eyes and tried activity
    Participated in activity and discussion
    Participated in activity and discussion. Gave two thoughtful examples.
    Participated in activity and discussion. Gave four insightful examples.

Activity 2
Biography of Louis Braille

    Little evidence of book being read
    Some evidence of book being read
    Excellent evidence of book being read

Activity 3
Demonstration of everyday activities

    Looked at Web page

    Looked at Web page and demonstrated two examples

    Showed evidence of reading Web page by demonstrating three examples

    Showed evidence of reading Web page by a superior demonstration of three or more examples

Activity 4
Uses of Braille

    Listed only 1 use
    Listed a few
    Listed 10 or more

FIGURE 8.1   Continued

Activity 5

Design an invention and make a model to ease everyday life for people with visual impairments.

> The student presents an original design, but has no model and description is unclear and unfocused.

> The student presents an original design and describes it clearly, but provides no model (or provides a model but the description of how it works is unclear or unfocused).

> The student presents an original design, describes its use clearly, and provides a model to show how it works.

CONCLUSION

Now you better understand how it is to be blind and how it would be to use Braille to read and write. Can people with visual impairment do more things than you thought before you went on this webquest? Have you seen Braille on signs and other places? Can you write your name in Braille, using the chart at the top of the webquest? To find out more about blindness, visit these Internet sites:

- Bits of Braille
  http://www.viterbo.edu/academic/ug/education/edu250/mmtryggestad1.htm
- Louis Braille Biographies
  http://www.nyise.org/braille.htm#louis

RESEARCH SKILLS FOR STUDENTS

In Figure 8.1, students are guided by the teacher to specific Web sites for particular activities, from which they must generate a new invention and new ideas based on their experience of being blind. Once students are proficient in locating and utilizing sites that the teacher has provided, the next step is to give the students strategies and tools to locate their own Web sites for their research questions, using keyword searches and logical operators.

Logical operators are based on Boolean logic, which is based on algebraic set theory. Teaching students how to use "and," "or," "not," or "near" between between two key words will expand the power of their searching capabilities as well as increase their understanding of Venn diagrams and attribute theory!

Teachers also need to help students learn how to keep track of what they've found. In traditional classrooms, students were taught to use index cards to laboriously record quotations, citations, and information by hand. Now students need skills in creating databases or cluster diagrams to organize their information. (See Chapter 2 for more information on databases.) Figure 8.2 shows how a simple database might be organized for research.

FIGURE 8.2   Database for Storing/Retrieving Information

Source: (Author, Title, Date, URL)

Subject:

Keywords:

Abstract:

RESEARCH RESOURCES FOR TEACHERS AND PARENTS

In addition to the search engines that index Web pages and can empower (and sometimes overwhelm) the user, the development of distance learning resources at libraries and universities also provides help to teachers and families looking for information. At San José State University, for example, all faculty and students have access to abstracts and journals on-line. That is, when a student needs to read a journal article on a particular topic, or a faculty member wants to review research to write a journal article, grant, or book, they can use passwords to get on-line access directly to the journals to which the library subscribes.

BOOKMARKS

Browsers provide users with a way of marking frequently used Web sites with an electronic "bookmark" so that it is not necessary to keep track of lengthy Web site addresses. Many teachers and parents mark the sites of frequently used search engines (i.e., *www.google.com, www.yahooligans.com*) so that, when a research project is assigned, students move quickly and easily to the start of their search.

KEYPALS

Goldsworthy (1999/2000) describes a typical class project that utilizes the Internet and the development of keypals in locations across the country and worldwide:

A group of students comes in from outside. They are carrying a set of tools, one of which looks like a thermometer, another some sort of sock, and yet another a clipboard. The group members sit down around a computer workstation and busily type in something, discuss among themselves for a moment, then return to their seats.

Later, one of the students, perhaps it was the one carrying the thermometer, reports to the entire class that it looks as though it'll be an early winter in Colorado and that we shouldn't be surprised if it rains tomorrow. These students are involved in a collaborative activity with five other classrooms around the country. They begin each class by gathering such meteorological data from their area as rainfall amount, temperature, and wind direction and approximate velocity.

This information is sent to each of the other five teams. They are responsible for reporting the data to the other teams before the end of the day, and they expect to receive the data from each of the other teams by the next morning. When the students receive the information from their peers, they enter it into the database they designed themselves. This database allows them to track changes in the weather across time and location and begin to observe weather patterns across the country. In this case, the group also has a map that may be written on with dry-erase markers, and they post the weather information as it comes in.

All of the information is passed between groups with nothing more than an e-mail account at each location. What is more, the students at each location frequently start conversations with one another and grow, therefore, not only in their understanding of science and mathematics but writing as well. They are motivated to write, and write well, to an audience of their peers. Additionally, the within-group and across-group collaboration fosters intrapersonal and interpersonal understanding (p. 6).

Burkhart and Kelly (1999) offer several tips for teachers who want to experiment with keypals in their classrooms:

1. Teachers may want to begin with class-to-class E-mails, through their own E-mail accounts, so messages can be screened, and so that the risk of having one or two children without a response, or difficulties with absences, can be minimized.
2. Some teachers may want to have their class write "cliff hangers" and invite the other class to write an ending.
3. Students can do parallel science experiments or conduct surveys.
4. Students can read the same book and share ideas or responses (an electronic literature circle).

Some resources for E-mail services especially designed for classroom use include *www.gaggle.net* (a free E-mail service with teacher controls and filters and kid-safe advertisements), and Classroom Connect (*www.classroom.net/teachercontact*)

ELECTRONIC MENTORING

Students can also take advantage of the expertise of leading scientists through electronic mentoring. Hewlett-Packard, for example, sponsors a Telementor Program (*www.telementor. org/hp/*), which matches employees with K–12 student apprentices throughout the world. In the 1996–1997 academic year, more than 1,500 employees participated in the program. Another mentoring project, The Electronic Emissary (*www.tapr.org/emissary*), matches subject matter experts and students or groups of students. Emissary volunteers also help coordinate the exchanges (Roblyer & Edwards, 2000). For teachers, students, and parents who are working on space-related projects, Quest: NASA K–12 Internet Initiative (*http:// quest.arc.nasa.gov*) houses several wonderful NASA-supported projects, such as broadcasts, scheduled chat events, and on-line materials. Recent hot topics include the brain's functioning in microgravity (Neuron), the Mars pathfinder mission, and shuttle flights. Those seeking to pose questions during interactive chat sessions with NASA scientists should check the schedule (*http://quest.arc.nasa.gov/common/events*) regularly because only the first 25 to register are usually permitted to post questions (Goldsworthy, 1999/2000).

Students can publish the results of their work through a project such KidPub WWW Publishing (*www.kidpub.org/kidpub*). Literally thousands of stories and other artifacts have been published by children.

ELECTRONIC (VIRTUAL) FIELD TRIPS

Electronic field trips enable students, families, and teachers to go places they've never been, without leaving their homes or classrooms! While not taking the place of real travel experiences, electronic field trips provide an opportunity to explore unique locations around the world and to share that experience with each other (Roblyer & Edwards, 2000). Students might visit their state capitol electronically during the legislative session, for example, and interact with their local legislator by E-mail. They can also journey to the Amazon and correspond with scientists on an archeological dig or search to find medicinal herbs (e.g., the Jason project). Trena Bradley (2001), teacher of young students with severe physical disabilities, describes an electronic field trip to see some animals in the zoo and in their natural habitats:

> I introduced the zoo animals. I started off by showing them a picture and then they had to say or sign the name. After they named the animals, they got to choose one and go on a guided tour with me. We then went to *www.nationalgeographic.com*, and then to *www. discovery.com*, and found pictures of the animals they identified. We also tried *www. animalplanet.com*, and there were live cameras hooked up. The students could watch the animals in their natural environment or in their zoo pens. They then had to count the number of animals on the screen and tell me what color their animals were. I went further with some of my students and they could tell me where they lived—in a tree, in the jungle. This was exciting for the students! You should have heard the giggles and oh's and ah's when they watched the lion yawn or the elephant spray water. I had fun, and the children appeared to enjoy it as well.

Burkhart and Kelly's suggestions (1999) for enhancing virtual field trips include:

1. Prior to the virtual field trip, students could read about the place in books or articles and formulate questions about the place they are about to visit;
2. Use a projector or TV to enlarge the computer screen, and have the students take turns controlling the mouse as the class participates in a discussion of what you find;

3. Leave the Web site up during writing time so that students can refresh their memories and check information as needed;
4. Following the field trip, students can compare what they learned to what they had found in books and articles.

An example of a virtual historical field trip is "You Be the Historian" at *http://americanhistory.si.edu/hohr/springer,* in which students discover what life was like 200 years ago for a family in Delaware. Students can generate questions about what life was like prior to the field trip. They can then use items found in the house as clues to discover information about the family and their daily lives.

DISCUSSION GROUPS

Many Internet service providers offer a way to set up an electronic bulletin board or discussion board. The teacher can post a question, journal prompt, or issue, and students can post their responses, to the prompt, to each other, or both! The teacher can join in the discussion, too; the quality of the discussion helps the teacher gain insight into the depth of student understanding of classroom projects, issues, and activities.

ON-LINE PROJECTS

An excellent way to become familiar with structuring on-line projects on the Internet is to join one that addresses your curriculum objectives that someone else has set up. You can extend the project with activities that are geared to your students' learning needs. In the area of science, for example, two such projects include:

- Athena-Earth and Space Science for K–12: Oceans, Earth, Weather, and Space (*http://www.athena.ivv.nasa.gov*). Students and teachers can use data and participate in ongoing experiments with data provided by NASA.
- NASA Classroom of the Future: Exploring the Environment. Students grapple with problems currently being investigated by practicing scientists and manipulate actual data relevant to these problems. This series has 17 Web-based learning modules that use NASA on-line imaging data to investigate problems. Each module begins with a situation, such as a volcano eruption, a hurricane, or the diminishing rain forest.
- The Ocean Planet: Smithsonian Traveling (*http://www.smithsonian.org*) An on-line version of the actual traveling exhibition that draws attention the world's oceans. Interdisciplinary lesson plans and materials and activities to practice math and writing are available on line.

Two sites that provide listings of on-line projects are: *http://www.eduplace.com/projects* and *http://archives.gsn.org/hilites/index.shtml.*

Once you've participated in an ongoing project designed by someone else, you will probably be ready to set up your own project. Several Web sites are available to link teachers who are interested in participating in on-line projects:

http://connectedteacher.classroom.com/home.asp
http://www.stolaf.edu/network/iecc
http://web66.coled.umn.edu/schools.html

SAFETY ISSUES ON THE INTERNET

While the Internet is a wonderful opportunity for learning and provides vital connections to the world, it is not without risks. Parents and school personnel will want to protect students from inappropriate encounters and follow simple guidelines for safety, such as the following (Gardner, 1996):

1. keep an eye on students while they are using the Internet;
2. send an agreement home for parents to sign explaining the benefits and risks of using the internet;
3. Create a list of Internet sites that are safe and bookmark them;
4. do not post personal information about anyone;
5. do not give out your home phone number or your address to anyone.

STUDENT ACTIVITIES

1. Make a list of ten ways you can increase student learning or engagement using Web-supported activities.

2. Visit the Webquest matrix site and select a Webquest to try with your students (*http://edweb. sdsu.edu/webquest/matrix.html*). Write up a reflection on the impact of the Webquest on your students' learning and engagement.

3. Observe a classroom where a teacher is using the Internet to link students with their counterparts in another part of the country or world. Interview the teacher and a student to find out (1) the benefits of such connections, and (2) the challenges.

REFERENCES

Becker, H. (1998). Running to catch a moving train: Schools and information technology. *Theory into Practice, 35*(1), 20–30.

Bradley, T. (2001). Unpublished project for SPED 346C, California State University, Chico.

Burkhart, L., & Kelly, K. (1999). Using the Internet in elementary and middle school classrooms. [On-line]. Avialable at: *http://www.Lburkhart.com*

CAST. (2000). The role of online communications in schools: A National Study. [On-line]. Available at: *http://www.cast.org*

Forcier, R. (1999). *The computer as an educational tool: Productivity and problem-solving.* Upper Saddle River, NJ: Merrill/Prentice-Hall.

Gardner, P. (1996). Internet for teachers and parents. Huntington Beach, CA: Teachers Created Materials, Inc.

Goldsworthy, R. (1999/2000). Collaborative classrooms. *Learning and Leading with Technology, 27*(4), 6–9.

Mackenzie, J. (2000). *Beyond technology: Questioning, research, and the information literate school.* Bellingham, WA: FNO Press.

Papert, S. (1996). *The connected family: Bridging the digital generation gap.* Marietta, GA: Longstreet Press.

Pineo, M. (2001). Unpublished project for SPED 346C, California State University, Chico.

Roblyer, M., & Edwards, J. (2000). *Integrating educational technology into teaching.* Upper Saddle River, NJ: Prentice-Hall.

Tapscott, D. (1999). Educating the net generation. *Educational leadership. 56*(5), 6–11.

CHAPTER NINE

CREATING YOUR OWN WEB SITES AND WEB PAGES

Most teachers have adopted the use of the Internet as a source of information, either to find out information for themselves or for parents; many teachers also enjoy the resources of the Internet for classroom projects, as described in Chapter 8. In this chapter, we look at the empowering aspects of developing and maintaining a Web site at the classroom, school, and/or district level. Some of the questions posed by the chapter include:

- Why would a teacher, school, or program want to design/maintain a Web site?
- What is involved in Web site development, and what roles do teachers, parents, and students play?
- What would a successful classroom, school, or district Web site look like, and how would we know one if we saw it?
- What, exactly, makes a Web site "empowering"?
- Are there special considerations for accessibility we, as special educators, must consider as we think about developing our own Web sites?

CHAPTER GOALS

When you've completed this chapter, you will have:

1. listed the reasons to develop a Web site or evaluate the Web site you have;
2. explored school/program Web sites and evaluated their usefulness and appeal;
3. considered universal design aspects of Web site design and found out how to evaluate your Web site for accessibility.

BENEFITS OF A CLASSROOM/SCHOOL/DISTRICT WEB SITE

According to McKenzie (1997), four goals form the basis for a school or district to create a Web site. A high quality Web site:

1. introduces the school to the community and the world: its mission, character, its look, its offerings for children, and its overall spirit. In an era when schools feel victimized by media portrayals of their weaknesses, a high quality Web site gives a school a chance to highlight its strengths and to present data and information in a way not available in other media;

2. points to excellent information on the Web: identifies the best resources the Web has to offer their families and students, resources that support the curriculum and the kinds of investigations likely to be undertaken by staff and students alike. The kinds of projects and internet resources visible on a school's Web site illustrate the types of learning and teaching available in the schools and helps students and families get the most from their time on the Internet;

3. offers students the opportunity to publish their work (art, music, writing) for a local and global audience;

4. provides rich, locally collected data on curriculum-related topics (such as local history), in the form of virtual museums, libraries, or data warehouses.

Additional benefits of a high quality Web site, according to Hixson and Schrock (1998), include enhancing home–school communication and facilitating communication among staff and students. A school Web site can help teachers and students focus on and evaluate information by providing such resources as a hotlist (useful Web links), a multimedia scrapbook (links to photographs, maps, videos, sounds, files, stories, facts, quotations, etc.), a treasure hunt (key questions about a topic and Web resources that hold the answers, to pique student and parent interest in an upcoming topic or event), a subject sampler (links to Web sites organized around a main topic with Web activities to respond to from a personal perspective, and webquests (explained in Chapter 8).

Not only can a school Web site help students publish and benefit from an audience for their work, but teachers have a chance to publish their lessons, activities, and helpful resources they have discovered on the Internet. Teachers who have a clear vision of the importance of project-based learning and student-centered approaches to teaching and learning find that the Internet helps students extend, transfer, and apply their skills in novel ways. "You want kids to yell 'I can know that!' and set off to pursue the question from multiple perspectives and publish the results—for the world to see," comments Lloyd Tabb, parent and volunteer teacher at Gateway School in Santa Cruz (he built the Webpage creation tool, Netscape Composer, and co-created the browser *mozilla.org*) and developer of *everyschool.org*, a free software program for schools to develop their student-centered Web sites (Cleary, 2001). "Teachers use Harvey [the Gateway Web site; see Figure 9.1] to give homework assignments and reminders. Students post their work where instructors and peers can review and comment on it. Parents can check on classwork or class activities. Grandparents have even peeked in to laud kids' projects," (Cleary, 2001). Harvey was developed primarily to see the impact of an expanded audience on student writing. Teachers began with the question, "If you give a student an expanded audience for their writing, will their writing improve? Tabb relates the experience of a sixth grader who went to a local bakery and ran into his kindergarten teacher, who called out to him, "Hey, I read the story you wrote! It was terrific!" Having an environment where teachers can stay

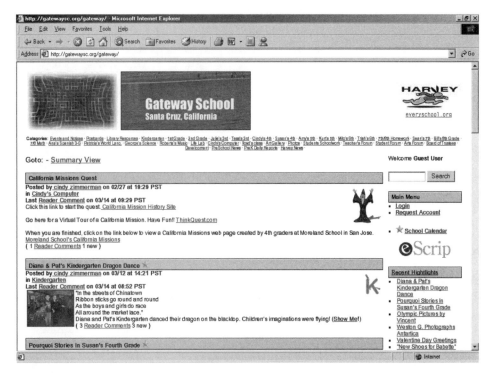

FIGURE 9.1 Gateway School's Harvey Web Site

in touch with their students' work from one year to the next, and where anyone who is interested in a student's work can stay plugged in, has had an incredible impact according to Tabb (personal communication, 2001). "Kids' writing just jumps through the roof: kids write, and they write well!" Similar "teaching moments" are captured in the WestEd Tales site (Figure 9.2).

Amy Rickerson's (2001) Web page, Figure 9.3, highlights her students' experiences in writing haiku and gives her a chance to share her experience, as she watches their skills develop.

QUESTIONS TO CONSIDER BEFORE LAUNCHING A WEB SITE DESIGN PROJECT

Do the benefits outweigh the costs?

The first question to consider, of course, is whether the costs of investing time and money in a high quality class, school, or district Web site development project are balanced by the perceived benefits. Tabb cautions: "The focus has to be on the teachers and the kids. Teachers and kids have to seek out the opportunity, and they have to stay at the center, or it won't work. It just can't come from the top down." Evidence of the validity of his experience comes

FIGURE 9.2   WestEd's Tales Web Site

quickly as one reviews the directory of school Web sites on Web 66 (*www.web66.coled. umn.edu*). There are many "dead" Web sites as evidenced by the messages "last updated June, 1998" or "site not found."

The most important benefit of a classroom, school, or district Web site, then, is the potential impact of such a site on student achievement. It can provide students with the opportunity to display portfolios of their work, motivate them to read and write more as they see their work published on-line, and give them the opportunity to develop technical skills as they learn more about computer networks and participate in writing Web content and Web pages.

Beyond the potential for student achievement, some practical ways that a Web site (Hixson & Schrock, 1998) can sustain a dialogue between school and community include posting important dates (events, school calendar, parent conference sign-up information, E-mail access to teachers), publicizing business items of interest to the community (vision/ mission statements, committee membership/activities, and volunteer opportunities), and newsletters.

A school Web site offers the opportunity to create a living picture of your school and to generate community support for the projects and activities that students undertake. The Web site becomes a focus for staff, parents, and students to work for improvement and success as participation in the shared vision unfolds.

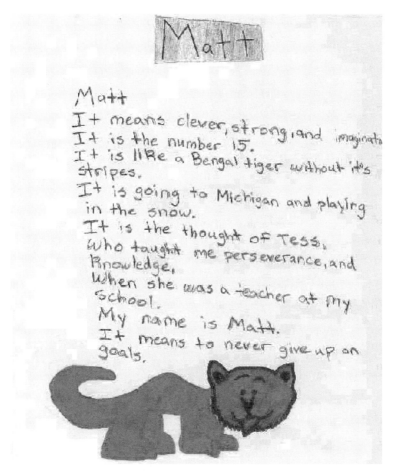

Matt

Matt
It means clever, strong, and imaginat
It is the number 15.
It is like a Bengal tiger without it's stripes.
It is going to Michigan and playing in the snow.
It is the thought of Tess, who taught me perseverance, and knowledge,
When she was a teacher at my school.
My name is Matt.
It means to never give up an goals.

FIGURE 9.3   Classroom Web Page

Whose Job Is It?

Designing and maintaining a Web site is a demanding job, and many decisions must be made about who will be responsible. Who makes the decisions about what is appropriate to post? What are school policies about parent permission for student photos and posting of student work? Who makes sure that copyright issues are reviewed and upheld? How are students identified? First names, or initials, or no names with pictures? How are students in special education designated in school or class Web pages?

Having a primary person responsible for developing and updating information is simple, but what if that person leaves? How invested do others feel in the continuation of the effort? To what degree should training and activities in Web site development be available to interested staff and parents? Who coordinates this effort? What technical support is available to maintain servers and the hardware necessary for optimum Web site operation? All of these questions suggest a thoughtful, ongoing examination of the issues by the people most directly involved: teachers, students, and parents.

HOW TO GET STARTED

Tabb is working currently with 30 schools all over the world that have downloaded the free Web site software from *www.everyday.org* (Linux server required). He offers the following suggestions:

1. Start small. Don't start schoolwide.
2. Begin with a pilot, with individual teachers who design a page using Web sites such as *www.tripod.com* or *www.geocities.com* to publish student work.
3. Start with what the kids are interested in; they'll figure it out.
4. Find someone in the community who's strong in technology and engage that person to work with the students.

Tabb describes his experience in an elective course with Gateway eighth graders.

"We began with a question: What is something useful we could provide for the community using technology? The kids came up with the idea of a teens' guide to Santa Cruz. The students would each contribute articles, artwork, and photographs for the site. The students decided on a name for the site, *roosters.com,* and the school purchased the domain name. Instead of a formal class, the students met in teams. They learned different skills, and they learned to respect what each person brought to the project. The key is to achieve real things with real tools—these are skills that will transfer to other educational settings and in the real world, and they clearly engage the student. The level of excitement, sense of ownership and autonomy were gratifying."

SPECIAL CONSIDERATIONS FOR ACCESSIBILITY

While the Internet is an incredible tool for providing access to information and resources beyond our wildest dreams, it can also pose barriers just as real as the architectural barriers that prevent access to buildings and roadways. As special educators, we must be leaders in the effort to make sure that our own Web sites are designed with universal access features in mind. The Center for Applied Technology (CAST) has designed a special tool to help Web page designers evaluate their work for accessibility. *Bobby* is a Web-based program that helps designers make sites accessible to the largest possible number of people, including those with disabilities. Bobby identifies accessibility problems on Web pages and teaches designers how to correct these problems so that their sites are more accessible. It also illustrates how Web pages will look via different browsers. For example, having a "text-only" version of each page of a Web site makes accessibility much easier for a person with visual impairment to access a page. On a page with graphics, each graphic can provide a text description. Figure 9.4 shows how a user submits a URL, which the program scans instantly, looking for typical troublesome accessibility features, then issues a report. When the page is successfully reviewed, the site receives a special "Bobby-approved" designation that can be posted on the site.

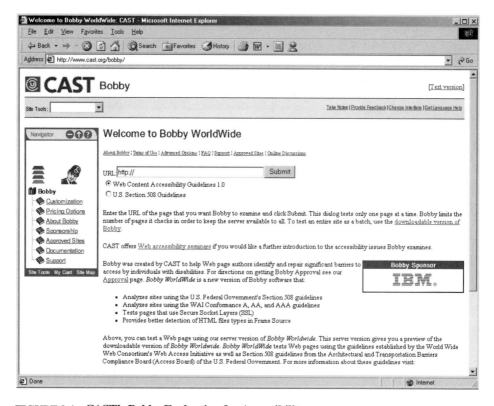

FIGURE 9.4   CAST's Bobby Evaluation for Accessibility

WHAT IS INVOLVED IN WEB SITE DESIGN?

Web pages are written in HyperText Markup Language (HTML), whose coding tells the browser how to display the file referenced on the page. Graphics are coded as separate files and saved so that the browser can find them. Text must also be coded for formatting features such as font, alignment, and so on. Unless you want to learn HTML, most Web page designers begin with a template (start with a page created by someone else and adapt it) or use a Web page editing program such as Dreamweaver, Claris Home Page, Microsoft Front Page, or Adobe Page Mill.

Web page editors take out the necessity of learning HTML, but that also takes away the power that comes with mastering the language behind Web page design. As your skills increase with editors, you can begin to learn the basics of HTML, which will make it easier to modify the pages and understand how the pages work. Roblyer and Edwards (2000) suggest the following steps in designing your own Web page:

1. Visit lots of Web pages, print them out, and print the source code for the ones you like.
2. Start with Inspiration to map out your site or use storyboards for each page.
3. Develop pages with text.
4. Insert images and sounds using a digital camera and scanned images, photos, or student artwork.
5. Insert links to other parts of the Web site or other Web sites that are relevant and useful for your audience/community.
6. Insert interactive elements, such as an opportunity to E-mail and to comment on the items posted.
7. Test your Web page in a browser such as Netscape Navigator or Internet Explorer.
8. Publish/upload the site.

    Web pages go onto a server (a computer that is always hooked up to the Internet, and set up to display the page to anyone who accesses it). In order to publish your page, you must find out how to access your school or district site and its policies/procedures or use your own Internet Service Provider (ISP) account (most commercial providers allow up to five megabytes of storage to post a personal or educational page without charge, such as AOL Hometown or Yahoo Geocities).

    You will need software to upload your page. FETCH for Mac or WS_FTP for IBM are two public-domain software programs that can be used.
9. Gather evaluation comments, revise, and maintain the site.

Figure 9.5 is a sample of an evaluation form used to critique and improve a Web site (Roblyer & Edwards, 2000).

ANNOUNCING YOUR WEB PAGE TO THE WORLD

Once your Web page has been successfully uploaded and you've had a chance to get evaluation feedback from users, you may want to let the world know you exist! You might begin by going to search engines you like and look for a link with directions about how to register your Web page such as the one in Figure 9.6 above from the Google search engine Web site.

You can register with Web66 (*http://web66.coled.umn.edu/schools*), a directory of school Web sites, shown in Figure 9.7.

You can also post it on a listserv (a mailing list that sends the same message to the members on the list) or an educational mailing list. You can also E-mail the links that you have on your Web site, give them your Web site, and let them know that you are using a link to their Web site as part of your program. Many sites will voluntarily include a link back to you (Payton, 1997).

FIGURE 9.5   Web Site Evaluation Form

Content

____ All information is accurate; plan to update the page periodically. The "last time updated" date is given.

____ Information is complete but not excessive or redundant.

____ Information is well-organized and clearly labeled.

____ Information is interesting, informative, and worthwhile.

____ Information is not redundant to many other sources; there is a reason to put it on the Web.

____ Level of content and vocabulary are appropriate for intended audience.

____ Content is free from stereotyping, course or vulgar language, or matter that could be offensive to typical users.

____ Author(s) of the page are clearly identified.

____ The page gives an E-mail address or other way to contact authors.

____ Universal design features are built into the site so that the site is accessible by users with visual impairments, physical disabilities, etc. (Bobby designation)

Visual and Audio Design

____ The site has a consistent look.

____ Graphics, animations, videos, and sounds make an important contribution; each serves a purpose.

____ Pages have only one or two fonts.

____ Each page uses a limited number of colors, especially for text.

____ Colors have been selected to be compatible with the Netscape 216 Color palette.

____ Type colors/styles and text-to-background contrast have been selected for good readability.

____ Each graphic is designed to fit 640×480 pixel screens, allowing for scroll bars/toolbars.

____ Each page is limited to 2–3 screens; the most important information is at the top.

____ The pages are simply and attractively designed; they make a user want to read the information.

____ The page has been submitted to Bobby and universal design features such as a "text-only" version of the page(s) are available.

Navigation

____ Pages load quickly.

(continued)

FIGURE 9.5   Continueda

___ Pages have a simple, consistent navigation scheme to let users get to desired places quickly and easily.

___ The first page indicates clearly how the site is organized and how to get to items of interest.

___ Links (text and icons) are easy to identify. Graphics and sounds are clearly identified.

___ Icons clearly represent the information they link to.

___ Each supporting page has a link back to the home page.

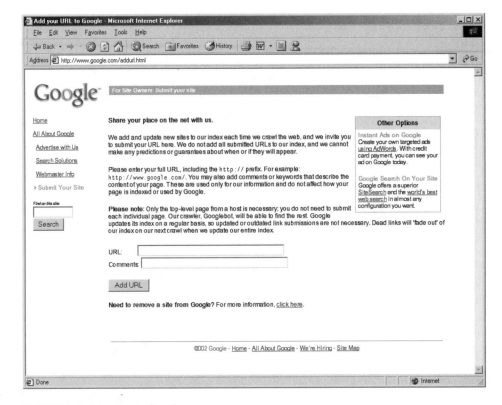

FIGURE 9.6   Linking to Google

USING/CREATING WEB MUSEUMS

According to Hill, (*http://rims.k12.ca.us/score_lessons/cue/history_geography.htm*), Web museums are "visually rich presentations of information organized according to themes in the manner of a museum." Web museums can include such resources as paintings and

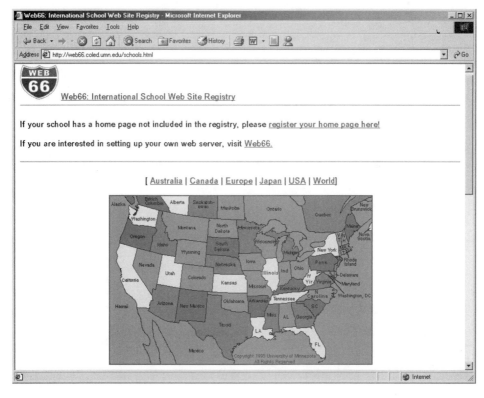

FIGURE 9.7   Web 66 Directory of School Web Sites

drawings, cartoons and photos, diagrams and graphs, maps, and brief text. Figure 9.8 shows an example of a Web museum organized around regions or environments. With a digital camera, or using digital resources available on the Web, teachers and students can construct their own Web museum sites.

STUDENT ACTIVITIES

1. Visit the Gateway School Web site. Make a list of five ways in which such a Web site might improve school–family–student–community communication.

2. Using a Web page authoring tool (Publisher, Home Page, DreamWeaver, etc.), design a Web page for your classroom. Evaluate it using the evaluation form in the chapter. List the ways in which students and families are empowered by visiting the site.

3. Visit the the SCORE Web Museum site. *http://rims.k12.ca.us/score_lessons/cue/history_ geography.htm.* List five ideas for how you might use a Web museum to help students learn about your community.

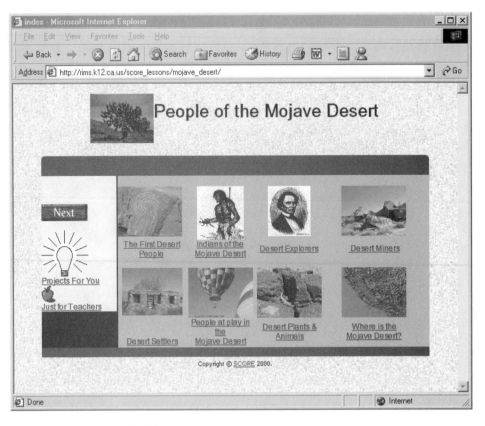

FIGURE 9.8   Example of a Web Museum

REFERENCES

Cleary, S. (March 28, 2001). Valley veteran wants to show high-tech has role in classroom. *Wall Street Journal. http://everyschool.org/u/harvey/lloyd.tabb/wsjharvey.htm.*

Hill, M. (no date). Web Museums Oral History Interviews, and Classroom Exchanges. Technology to Teach Local History and Geography. *http://rims.k12.ca.us/score_lessons/cue/history_geography.htm*

Hixson, S., & Schrock, K. (1998). *Developing Web pages for school and classroom.* Westminster, CA: Teacher Created Materials.

McKenzie, J. (1997). Why in the World Wide Web? *From Now On, 6*(6), www.fno.com

Payton, T. (1997). Announcing your Web page. *http://www.siec.k12.in.us/~west /online/announce.htm*

Roblyer, M., & Edwards, J. (2000). *Integrating educational technology into teaching.* Upper Saddle River, NJ: Merrill.

CHAPTER TEN

VIRTUAL REALITY

Imagine being able to step outside one's everyday school or home environment to experience a world free of the limits and constraints of reality! We've seen it in the movies, amusement parks, and in science fiction television shows. Researchers are finding powerful applications for students with disabilities harnessing the power of the virtual reality environment. Virtual reality is "a computer-based technology that creates an illusion of reality, in which the participants interact with, and in fact are immersed in, an artificial environment to the degree that it appears real; it is highly interactive, multi-sensory, and vivid enough for the participants almost to think it is reality" (Forcier, 1999, p. 80).

In this chapter, you will have the opportunity to explore the possibilities of the virtual reality learning environments for your students.

CHAPTER GOALS

After completing this chapter, you will have explored:

1. what virtual reality means;
2. situations in which virtual reality might be appropriate for your students and examples of successful virtual reality studies with students of differing abilities;
3. resources for virtual reality tools and software.

HOW DOES VIRTUAL REALITY WORK?

Many of us are familiar with the low-end virtual reality experiences of computer games and simulations such as "The Sims," "Myst," and the like, where we wander through environments and make decisions about what to do next. Others of us have ridden an amusement park ride while sitting in a theater, with seats that move slightly, giving us the actual feeling of riding in a Formula One race car or careening down a roller coaster slope as we watch the images on a movie screen. At the high end, the user might wear a helmet or head-mounted display with special sensors, attached to sensor-equipped gloves or even a full body suit. The sensors give feedback to the computer so that ongoing environmental modification is possible.

The helmet positions video images and sounds for the viewer's eyes and ears, so that all other visual and auditory stimuli are blocked out. The viewer experiences realistic, 3-D images, and the responses of the user create a feedback loop with the computer, which makes an individualized experience for each user possible (Forcier, 1999). Although the high cost of virtual reality technology has largely kept it out of K–12 education, prices continue to drop. "It is estimated that fully immersive virtual reality will be affordable for schools within the next five years" (Wall, cited in Sprague, 1996). Before leaping on the technology bandwagon, however, teachers need to consider what has been learned from early virtual reality research.

CHARACTERISTICS OF VIRTUAL REALITY THAT BENEFIT STUDENTS WITH SPECIAL NEEDS

Darrow and Powers (1996) identify the characteristics of virtual reality that offer the greatest promise for the success of students with special needs:

- *Modeling, cueing, and shaping.* Virtual reality offers the benefit of a built-in coach, with different levels of scaffolding that can be designed into the environment, then faded as the student develops needed skills progressively. As Fritz (1991, p. 46) describes it, the learner can "superimpose his [or her] hand over the hand of an expert and follow along."
- *Flexibility.* Imagine learning to play the piano in an environment in which the notes are highlighted, and the notes you play are highlighted in a different color. As the developing musician becomes more proficient, the notes coalesce, and the music becomes pleasanter to the ear.
- *Realism.* With the 3-D lifelike images available in virtual reality, students can venture into environments that are too difficult logistically, or for safety reasons, to provide within the context of the school day. The virtual reality experiences can be alternated with real life to provide a seamless continuity between simulation and reality, for more frequent practice. As Stewart (1992) notes, "Virtual worlds aren't pictures, they're places. You don't observe them, you experience them" (p. 38).
- *Robotics.* People with physical disabilities can learn to control robotic devices in their environments, adapting them to do the tasks most significant for them, so that the devices they end up with are appropriately individualized and practical.
- *Sensory experiences.* Imagine the exhilaration of being able to experience physical movement for people who have little or no control of their body. With virtual reality, an eye blink can control a golf club or shoot a basket, and people in different places can join in a game simultaneously.

EXAMPLES OF VIRTUAL REALITY IN SPECIAL EDUCATION

In special education, virtual reality has been investigated for its usefulness primarily in the following areas (Roblyer & Cass, 1999):

1. rehabilitation of physical disabilities
2. wheelchair and mobility training

3. training activities for people with cognitive limitations or mental retardation
4. social skills and life skills activities for people with behavioral disorders and emotional disturbance
5. training activities for students with autism
6. flexible thinking training for students with hearing impairments

Although research in virtual reality applications for students with special needs is still in the early stages, results from studies offer much hope for the use of environments that may be safer, less intrusive, and provide more structure for practice than real-life situations.

In the physical rehabilitation field, people with physical disabilities have been helped to regain skilled movement. The virtual reality activities provide a safe environment in which persons with physical disability can expand their skills (Andrae, 1996; Kuhlen & Doyle, 1994; Latash, 1998; Rose, Johnson, & Attree, 1997).

At the Oregon Research Institute, students as young as three years old with cerebral palsy learn to operate a motorized wheelchair in a virtual reality environment. Students who had been unable to reliably operate a motorized wheelchair in their real-life homes and schools developed the skills necessary to navigate school corridors and sidewalks and around their homes and neighborhoods. The success of the outcomes for students are measured by their generalization to the real-world environment (Ira, 1997).

Using a virtual reality environment, researchers taught social skills to students with mental and behavior disorders by having them observe models, make choices provided in demonstrations, and practice initiating certain skills (Muscott & Gifford, 1994). Students with learning disabilities have also been successful in preliminary studies of virtual reality environments that teach living skills (Cromby, Standen, & Brown, 1995). Initial studies have had promising results; more long-term studies of generalization of the skills are needed. A virtual reality kitchen called "Softhaven" was used by researchers to help students with brain injury to relearn cooking skills. Softhaven provided a series of prompts and cues to help learners select the correct utensil needed for cooking. Through the structure of this virtual kitchen, students mastered skills quickly and reliably (Christiansen, Abreu, Ottenbacher, Huffman, Masel, & Culpepper, 1998).

Students with autism have been studied using virtual reality environments to help them learn to cross the street. In two case studies, children mastered the simple tasks and successfully took virtual walks and located objects in the environment. Because of the difficulty that students with autism have with processing multiple sources of input, it was thought that virtual reality systems might help them to isolate and control stimuli. Students with autism appear to respond readily to computer environments, and the use of virtual reality enables the teacher to make individual adjustments for each child's needs. Because researchers believe that students with autism are primarily "visual" thinkers, virtual reality capitalizes on this characteristic, making successful interventions more likely (Roblyer & Cass, 1999).

Deaf and hard-of-hearing students used a virtual reality environment (low-end) to increase the flexibility of their thinking in a non-verbal environment. Researchers have noted that deaf and hard-of-hearing students are typically taught in an environment that emphasizes their deficit areas in language, communication, and reading. Because of this emphasis, it is thought, other aspects of intellectual functioning are not developed. Given the close link between creativity and imagination, the ability to think flexibly is an important attribute. When deaf and hard-of-hearing students are compared to hearing students, their performance on flexible thinking tasks is lower. After the virtual reality experiment, using VR Tetris, no differences in flexible thinking were found between deaf and hard-of-hearing students and hearing students. The deaf and hard-of-hearing students in the control group, using a two-dimension version of Tetris, scored no differently on flexible thinking before and after the study. The researchers' explanation of the results focused on the nature of VR technology.

> This technology creates a 'presymbolic' form of communication, and its users can communicate with imaginary worlds without the use of words. Thus a world is created that is charged with sights, voices, and sensations that surpass syntax and language. The deaf and hard-of-hearing children who used this technology were able to realize their hidden potential without linguistic or auditory limitations. VR technology does not limit the player in either the manner in which information is presented or in his or her movements (Passig & Eden, 2000, p. 289).

PHYSICAL RISK-TAKING

One of the issues that may arise for students with physical disabilities is the development of a sort of passivity and dependence with regard to the world around them. Accustomed to limitations of movement and control over their environment, students with physical disabilities may not experience the empowerment that able-bodied persons do when engaged with their world. This attitude of passivity and dependence may also transfer to nonphysical activities if no intervention is undertaken.

With virtual reality, however, anyone can participate in activities that otherwise would be too expensive, too dangerous, or inappropriate to consider. With a harness and Dream Glider (Dreamality Technologies, Inc.), anyone can be a hang glider (Benno, 1998). Each ride is different, because the skills of the rider determine the course and length of the flight. Ultra Coaster allows users to design a roller coaster, using principles of physics and engineering, and then ride in the front seat of the car, experiencing the exhilaration of weightlessness from the safety of their own classroom, office, or bedroom.

INTELLECTUAL RISK-TAKING

Just as students with physical disabilities may become passive and dependent in their physical environment, students with learning disabilities may become fearful and unwilling to take risks in the learning environment due to their past punishing experiences with failure. In the virtual reality environment, students can conduct chemistry experiments, dissect frogs, explore volcanoes, and travel through space, unencumbered by the limitations of reading skills, empowered by the multisensory nature of the activities. "Various studies in the field of virtual reality have found that this immersion serves to broaden the interface with the senses and also improves the ability to understand abstract concepts by converting them to more concrete ones" (Passig & Segal, 2000, p. 290). We are only beginning to realize the power of the unique quality of virtual reality in activating and engaging the learner, moving from passive observer to active participant (Bricken & Byrne, 1992; Heim, 1992; Osberg, 1995; Powers & Darrow, 1996).

CREATING MENTAL MODELS

In reviewing the research on virtual reality across students, with and without disabilities, the preliminary outcomes, though still in formative stages, confirm the power of this technology. Studies of students using the virtual reality environments of NewtonWorld to explore the laws of motion, kinetic energy, and linear momentum; MaxwellWorld to explore the nature of electrostatic forces and fields, and PaulingWorld to explore the structure of small and large molecules from different viewpoints, show that:

1. the use of multisensory cues (visual, auditory, and haptic) engages learners and directs their attention to important behaviors and relationships;
2. new representations and perspectives help students transform and alter their misconceptions formed during traditional instruction;
3. multimodal interaction seems to enhance learning outcomes;
4. collaborative learning is enhanced when two or more students learn together, recording and guiding their virtual reality experience (Sprague, 1996).

IDEAS AND ACTIVITIES FOR VIRTUAL REALITY

For many teachers, virtual reality tools may seem beyond the reach of the typical school or classroom. These tools are seen more as an entertainment medium than an educational one. Here are some suggestions for getting started, keeping in mind how quickly the tools are developing and how rapidly costs are declining:

1. search for virtual reality software and tools at *www.google.com* for the latest products and information;
2. visit the Web sites in the next section to get your imagination engaged and to connect with other educators involved in virtual reality exploration;
3. try out some examples of virtual worlds software, for example, The Sims (Electronic Arts) and UltraCoaster (ReactorSoftware) on your own and with your students to explore this new type of learning.

RESOURCES IN VIRTUAL REALITY
FOR SPECIAL EDUCATORS

- *http://www.ori.org/educationvr.html*
  The Web site for the Oregon Research Institute provides abstracts of current research projects in virtual reality and contacts for further information.

- *http://www.hitl.washington.edu/kb/edvr/*
  This Web site provides information and resources from the Human Interface Technology Laboratory at the University of Washington.
- *http://www.soe.ecu.edu/vr/vpbib.html#Disabilities*
  This Web site provides a comprehensive bibliography of journal articles and information sources on Virtual Reality and Education: Information Sources edited by Veronica S. Pantelidis, Ph.D.
- *ftp://ftp.cs.ucf.edu/pub/ExploreNet*
  ExploreNet™ is a general-purpose object oriented, distributed two-dimensional graphic-based computational environment with features to support role-playing games for educational purposes, and cooperative learning of many kinds.
- *http://www.iss.nus.sg/RND/cs/idl/kidsover.html*
  KidSpace: Interactive Discovery Learning pilot implementation, a Singapore National Project for children, ages seven through eleven.
- *http://www.vetl.uh.edu/ScienceSpace/ScienceSpace.html*
- *http://www.virtual.gmu.edu/vrhome.htm*
  Project ScienceSpace is an ongoing series of controlled experiments to assess the potential impact of Virtual Reality in science education. The Project is a joint effort between the Virtual Environment Technology Laboratory (VETL) at STB-VR Lab at Johnson Space Center and George Mason University.
- *http://quoll.maneng.nott.ac.uk/Research/virart/educn/index.html*
  Nottingham, University of, Dept. of Manufacturing: Virtual Reality Applications Research Team (VIRART) Education Applications. VIRART has now been involved in the development and testing of virtual environments for students with severe learning difficulties for the last four years. The primary testing for this work has been the Shepherd School in Aspley, Nottingham.
- *http://www.ice.eecs.uic.edu/~nice*
  N.I.C.E. project: University of Illinois at Chicago. This is a learning environment for young children, implemented in the CAVE™ virtual reality environment. Children can collaboratively construct artifacts in the CAVE and, in doing so, build an underlying narrative that is driven by constructionism.

STUDENT ACTIVITIES

1. List three ideas for how virtual reality might be a valuable learning tool for your students, based on the reading and/or your own experience.

2. Visit one of the Web site resources on virtual reality listed in the chapter. List three useful ideas that you learned from visiting the site.

3. Why do you think virtual reality has such potential to help students with special needs?

REFERENCES

Andrae, M. (1996). Virtual reality in rehabilitation. *British Medical Journal International, 312*(7022), 4–5.
Benno, M. (1998). Virtual reality. *Gifted Child Today Magazine, 21,* 12–14.

Bricken, M., & Byrne, C. (1992). Summer student in virtual reality: A pilot study on educational applications of virtual reality technology. University of Washington HIT Lab. [On-line]. Available at: *http://www.hitl.washington.eduprojects/education/*

Christiansen, C., Abreu, K., Ottenbacher, K., Huffman, K., Masel, B., & Culpepper, R. (1998). Task performance in virtual environments used for cognitive rehabilitation after traumatic brain injury. *Archives of Physical Medicine and Rehabilitation, 79,* 888–892.

Cromby, J., Standen, P., & Brown, D. (1995). Using virtual environments in special education. VR in the Schools 1(3). [On-line serial]. Available at: *http://eastnet.educ.edu.edu/vr/vrits/1-3-cont.htm.*

Darrow, M., & Powers, D. (1996). A promising future for applications of virtual reality to special education best practices. Proceedings of the CSUN Center on Disabilities Virtual Reality Conference.

Forcier, R. (1999). *The computer as an educational tool: Productivity and problem-solving* (2nd ed.). Upper Saddle River, NJ: Prentice-Hall.

Fritz, M. (1991). The world of virtual reality. *Training, 28*(2), 45–47.

Heim, M. (1992). *The metaphysics of virtual reality.* New York: Oxford University Press.

Ira, V. (1997). Virtual reality and mobility skills. *Exceptional Parent, 27*(11), 50.

Kuhlen, T., & Doyle, C. (1994). Virtual reality for physically disabled people. *Computing in Biological Medicine, 25*(2), 205–211.

Latash, M. (1998). Virtual reality: A fascinating tool for motor rehabilitation: To be used with caution. *Disability and Rehabilitation, 20*(3), 104–105.

Muscott, H., & Gifford, T. (1994). Virtual reality and social skills training for students with behavioral disorders: Applications, challenges, and promising practices. *Education and Treatment of Children, 17*(4), 417–434.

Osberg, K. (1995). Virtual reality and education: Where imagination and experience meet. *VR in the Schools, 1*(2), 1–3.

Passig, D., & Eden, S. (2000). Improving flexible thinking in deaf and hard of hearing children with virtual reality technology. *American Annals of the Deaf, 145*(3), 286–291.

Powers, D., & Darrow, M. (1996). Special education and virtual reality: Challenges and possibilities. *Journal of Research on Computing in Education, 27*(1), 11–121.

Roblyer, M., & Cass, M. (1999). Still more potential than performance: Virtual reality research in special education. *Learning and Leading with Technology, 26*(8), 50–53.

Rose, F., Johnson, D., & Attree, E. (1997). Rehabilitation of the head-injured child: Basic research and new technology. *Pediatric Rehabilitation, 1*(1), 3–7.

Sprague, D. (1996). Virtual reality and precollege education: Where are we today? *Learning and Leading with Technology, 23,* 10–12.

Stewart, D. (1992). Through the looking glass into an artificial world—via computer simulation. *Smithsonian, 21*(10), 36–45.

CHAPTER ELEVEN

TECHNOLOGY AND SERVICE-LEARNING

One of the most powerful ways to promote the infusion of technology throughout the inclusive school is through the use of *service-learning*. Although many schools throughout the country have implemented a wide range of service-learning projects to enhance citizenship, academic achievement, and personal development, relatively few schools have used technology as a focus of service-learning projects. Students with disabilities are often viewed by others, or themselves, as dependent on others, on the receiving end of services. Service-learning, on the other hand, puts students with special needs in the role of service provider. When combined with technology, a high-status skill area, students with special needs can participate effectively in projects that highlight their technology skills, thus changing perceptions (their own and others') of them from people who are "needy" to that of capable providers. In this chapter, you'll explore the definition of service-learning, research-validated outcomes of service-learning on academic, behavioral, social, and personal development, indicators of quality in service-learning projects, sample technology/service-learning projects of students with special needs, and ideas for projects that might be appropriate in your school or community.

CHAPTER GOALS

In this chapter, you will:

1. review the elements in the definition of service-learning and identify these elements in existing service-learning projects in your school or community;
2. reflect on research results that support the implementation of high quality service-learning projects in schools and communities for a variety of outcomes;
3. identify the indicators of high quality service-learning projects;
4. review sample technology/service-learning projects for ideas that might be relevant to your own teaching/learning situation;
5. develop your own technology/service-learning project ideas.

WHAT IS SERVICE-LEARNING?

The National Service Act of 1993 defines service-learning as a method:

- under which students learn and develop through active participation in thoughtfully designed service experiences that meet actual community needs and that are coordinated in collaboration with the school and community;
- that is integrated into the students' academic curriculum and provides structured time for a student to think, talk, or write about what the student did and saw during the actual service activity;
- that provides students with opportunities to use newly acquired skills and knowledge in real-life situations in their own communities; and
- that enhances what is taught in school by extending student learning beyond the classroom and into the community (Muscott, 2000, p. 350).

While different groups may define service-learning in slightly different ways, depending on whether the focus is philosophical, curricular, or civic, most people would agree that service-learning includes active participation in carefully organized experiences that meet both learning and community needs and provides opportunities for structured reflection (Billig, 2000). In developing your own service-learning projects, having a clear definition of what service-learning is will help establish standards and evaluation criteria (Sigmon, 1994). Service-learning is different from volunteer programs because of the partnership and the mutuality of goals of the participants. Students in service-learning projects view themselves as learning partners, learning themselves as they assist others in learning.

INDICATORS OF HIGH QUALITY
SERVICE-LEARNING PROJECTS

Eleven essential elements characterize of the successful studies described in the research (National Service-Learning Cooperative, 1998):

- clear educational goals requiring application of concepts, content, and skills from the academic disciplines and involving students in the construction of their own knowledge;
- tasks that engage, challenge, and stretch students cognitively and developmentally;
- assessment to gauge student learning;
- projects that meet genuine community needs;
- ongoing formative and summative evaluation to see how well student needs and community needs were met;
- student input throughout the design and implementation of the project;
- diversity is valued and is demonstrated by its participants, its practice, and its outcomes;
- projects feature partnerships and collaborations between school and community;

- students receive training for all aspects of their service work, and understand the tasks, their roles, the skills and information needed for the task, and the need for sensitivity to the people they will be working with;
- multiple methods used to acknowledge, celebrate, and validate students' service work.

In the sample projects described in this chapter, you can identify these quality indicators. As you plan your own projects, you will want to make them part of the design and implementation.

RESEARCH ON SERVICE-LEARNING OUTCOMES

While controlled studies of service-learning are still limited, the overall number of studies with positive outcomes is too large to be ignored. Eight broad areas of impact have been identified, with numerous studies within each area to confirm the positive results.

Improved Personal Development

Students in high quality service-learning projects perceived themselves to be more socially competent, were more likely to treat one another kindly, and had improved self-esteem and self-efficacy. Students in service-learning projects showed an increased sense of responsibility to their school, and were less likely to be referred to the office for discipline problems. High school students in service-learning projects were less likely to become pregnant or to be arrested.

Service-learning projects resulted in students who were more trusting and more trustworthy, who were more successful in bonding with adults, and who felt more comfortable communicating with ethnically diverse groups. They also showed greater empathy and acceptance of cultural diversity.

Increased Sense of Civic Responsibility

Elementary and middle-school students in service-learning projects had a greater sense of their responsibility as citizens, while high school students were more likely to consider politics and morality in society and to think about how to create social change. Students at all levels were more likely to be aware of community needs and how they could make a difference in society. Follow-up studies showed that service-learning participants were more likely to continue to engage in community service activities and to vote 15 years after their participation in service-learning activities.

Improved Academic Learning

Performance on standardized measures of reading and language arts and math, grade-point averages, and attendance all were noted as outcomes of participation in service-learning projects. Students took more initiative and were more successful in problem-solving tasks following participation in service-learning projects. Student motivation and students' perception of their learning were higher in service-learning projects and activities than in their other classes.

Increased Career Skills and Aspirations

Students in service-learning projects developed positive work habits and attitudes, reported increased career and communication skills, and greater awareness of their career possibilities.

Impact on Schools

In schools with high quality service-learning projects, teachers and students developed a greater appreciation and respect for each other, an improved school climate, and reduced teacher turnover. In addition, conversations about improvements in educational services and how best to teach and learn become more frequent and deeper.

Impact on Communities

Service-learning projects in the community result in a greater appreciation of community members for its youth, and improved relationships between school and community are perceived by project participants as well.

SERVICE-LEARNING OUTCOMES FOR STUDENTS WITH DISABILITIES

Relatively little research has been conducted on service-learning projects specifically focusing on students with disabilities, and, unfortunately, much of the research on service-learning has been conducted in projects in which no students with special needs were included. However, the outcomes from projects that have focused on students with special needs are similar to the outcomes reported for all service-learning projects reported above. In one study, a group of middle-school students in special education participated in a cross-age reading program with students in a nearby elementary school. The middle-school students' reading skills improved, as did the younger students'. In addition, both groups of students developed improved self-esteem and a greater love of reading (Jennings, 2001). Another study matched middle-school students in special education with residents in a senior center to conduct interviews on different time periods in the seniors' lives. The students then developed biographical essays on their partners based on the interview results, and the essays were compiled into a book that was presented to the local library, the historical society, and the senior center.

Results of eleven studies of students with emotional/behavioral disorders showed that students gained in self-esteem, educational achievement, improved peer relationships, increased ability to express feelings, and performance on standardized achievement tests.

Clearly, the results across all students in an inclusive school support the effectiveness of service-learning. By carefully designing service-learning projects that utilize technology, we expect to achieve similar outcomes.

SAMPLE TECHNOLOGY/ SERVICE-LEARNING PROJECTS

Tom Hart/Jule Dahl, Chico, California   Thomas Hart, a special education teacher for students with emotional/behavioral disorders at a school in Chico, California, started with one service-learning project that has grown into a series of interlocking projects, based on student interest and school needs. The project began with the "Computers For Schools" program, an all-volunteer program in which participants can earn their own computer system after putting in 60 hours of service.

Students can earn their 60 hours in multiple ways: hauling scrap and boxes to the dumpsters, helping to unload the trucks that donations arrive in, stacking computers, cleaning equipment, and so forth. For students who are interested, the program will teach them, over time, how to clean, service, maintain, diagnose, repair, and build computer systems. Also, students can join in collection trips, when large trucks are driven to Sacramento or farther to pick up donations from such varied places such as the state Capitol, the California Department of Education, and the California Department of Transportation.

After launching the computer acquisition/repair program, Tom initiated a computer music program. He discovered the "Miracle Piano System," a true midi keyboard that interfaced with older DOS-based computers and taught piano skills starting at the beginner level and progressed to advanced levels. This project overlapped with the Computers For Schools project because that program tries to place computers in the county classrooms that will run modern-day applications. When older systems are donated, Tom and his students repair and rebuild them and place them in classrooms to be used with the midi keyboards. In this way, his students get additional hands-on experience with computer hardware and the school now has a budding music program.

The third project emerged when Tom observed Jule Dahl's pull-out resource room program at nearby Ponderosa School. Jule was teaching a combined sign-language and music program in which students learned the signed for the words being sung. Tom had a few students who had expressed an interest in becoming teachers someday, so he brought the students in to observe the classroom. Over time, they asked if they could participate in the sign-language signing. It was a match made in heaven! Tom's high school students had younger children they could mentor and support, without the typical conflicts of dealing with their peers; the younger students now had a "big brothers" and "big sisters" they could impress. Tom notes, "Those kids would grin like Cheshire cats when my students arrived with me; they would sit up extra straight to show how they, too were able to be like "high school kids."

Tom's students mentioned the piano and the computer programs in which they were involved, and Jule asked if perhaps they could develop a "sister-school" mentoring arrangement with Tom's class. Tom brought some keyboards over to Ponderosa, powered them up, and one of his students started to work with a younger student on learning basic songs. In this way, both students have an opportunity to build appropriate relationships: Tom's students have an opportunity to be in an instructional and leadership role, and both students gain an opportunity to interact as a constructive team.

The next development in this evolving service-learning arena was for all the students in both programs to plan and organize a presentation of the skills they have learned. The students do "Signing and Singing" at Ponderosa School and for local convalescent hospitals, accompanied by students from both classes using the MIDI keyboards to play live music for an audience. What a wonderful opportunity to blend technology, learning, problem solving, positive leadership, and fun!

Now Tom's students go to a weekly art class at Ponderosa. The activities range from simple paper-and-marker art to making models, and incorporate a digital camera, student artwork, and Powerpoint software to give the students an avenue to express themselves in multimedia. In addition to learning Powerpoint, all the students have opportunities to express themselves creatively, to enhance their problem-solving strategies as they build their presentations, and to use music they have composed (with MusicWrite software, students can play a tune, which is saved in a MIDI format that Powerpoint can use).

With all the art and music that the students have created, Tom and Jules' next project was to teach them the principles of Web-page design. Through the variety of activities from computer repair to music and art, students needed a place to post their work for all the world to share and enjoy. The two schools now participate jointly in the Computers for Schools program and make blended field trips to pick up and deliver the systems on which they work.

Web page design is an excellent way to foster mentoring, leadership, teaching, teamwork, problem-solving, and creative statement because it uses the entire range of options available with our mentoring program. The computer part enables the students to know how the system is working, the music part allows them to learn to play and record their own music, and the Web page is a place where their art and music can be posted for all the world to share and enjoy.

Unless one is designing a computer system, one does not actually have to be completely literate in order to clean, maintain, diagnose, service, repair, or build a computer. Tom's students bring computers to the Ponderosa classroom, and introduce the Ponderosa students to the Computers For Schools program through blended field trips (Hart, 2001).

Kristin Anderson, Chico, California   In Kristin's school, all fifth graders must do research and write a report on a state of their choice. Kristin, who is a resource teacher, used this assignment—a huge challenge for her students—to develop a technology/service-learning project in which her students taught students in other fifth grade classrooms how to use PowerPoint to present their research. Some of her six students were unmotivated and struggling with these reports. "The State Report is boring," according to Katlin, one of the Kristen's students. The research and writing aspects of the report are difficult, especially for students with learning disabilities.

First, Kristin asked her students if they would be interested in learning to use PowerPoint. She explained that they could meet after school in the computer lab next door to the

Resource Room. She discussed how the program works and how it could be used to make their state reports more interesting. The students were elated!

Next, the students and Kristin presented the idea to the three fifth-grade teachers, Mrs. Moseley, Mr. Larson, and Mr. Wesley, and they were enthusiastic about the idea as well. They offered the students extra credit for their PowerPoint presentations. Mr. Larson added that showing the presentations to their classmates would be a beneficial experience. They all agreed this was a great idea.

In addition, Kristin and her students provided a Saturday training workshop for families of the fifth graders, so that parents would understand the work that their children were doing. Every student had friends and family members who showed up, which was very encouraging.

The academic outcomes and IEP goals in this project included:

- technological skills
- word-processing skills
- graphic tools
- research skills
- Internet and presentation software skills
- cooperative learning
- family involvement
- confidence
- empowering the student

Students also developed fluency and decoding and reading accuracy skills, and demonstrated writing in paragraph form, punctuation, and capitalization skills as well. Recalling major points is also a goal in all the students' IEP's.

Kristin is thrilled by the outcome of this service-learning experience because her students also gained self-esteem from the fruits of their labor. PowerPoint was more than worth the effort she put forward. This was also a great opportunity to bond with the students and parents outside of the classroom setting. The six fifth-grade students gained confidence in their abilities and enjoyed the learning process. Kristin notes, "when service-learning projects are put in place to meet a need, the outcome can be marvelous."

A sample of a student's state report using PowerPoint is provided in Figure 11.1.

Susie Rigas, Sunnyvale, California Susie's work in Ellis Elementary School was in a special day class of fourth and fifth graders. Their academic goals were to learn how to conduct a survey and make a chart of the results. Susie, working with teacher Sharon Eilts, planned a service-learning project in which the special day-class students learned how to conduct the survey (on music preferences) with a general education fifth-grade class, collected and analyzed the data on the computer using a spreadsheet, interpreted the data using a bar graph, presented and explained the results to classmates and the fifth-grade class, and trained the fifth graders to make charts using the same procedures they had used.

The students in the special day class decided what songs the survey should include. They then interviewed and tallied the results on paper, before entering the data into the

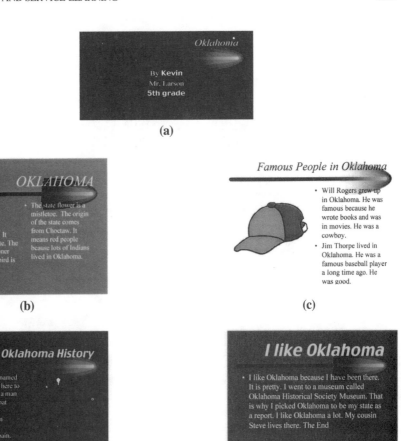

FIGURE 11.1   Kevin's State Report Using PowerPoint

spreadsheet. They decided that the data should include boys and girls as separate categories, so that gender music preferences could be explored. Figure 11.2 shows the results of the survey, and Figure 11.3 shows the music preference data in a bar graph.

TECHNOLOGY/SERVICE-LEARNING IDEAS AND RESOURCES

You may want to collect some resources before you start planning your first service-learning project. Where should you begin? Survey the school and the community for ways to make projects more interesting or less time-consuming by using technology.

Song	Artist	Girls	Boys
Drops of Jupiter	Train	3	5
Fallin'	Alicia Keys	3	0
I'm Like a Bird	Nelly Furtado	1	0
There You Be	Faith Hill	4	1
You Rock My World	Michael Jackson	3	8
Still	Brian McKnight	2	0
Shape of Heart	Backstreet Boys	10	3
Pop	NSYNC	8	9
Lady Marmalade	Various	3	8

FIGURE 11.2   Spreadsheet of Music Preference Data

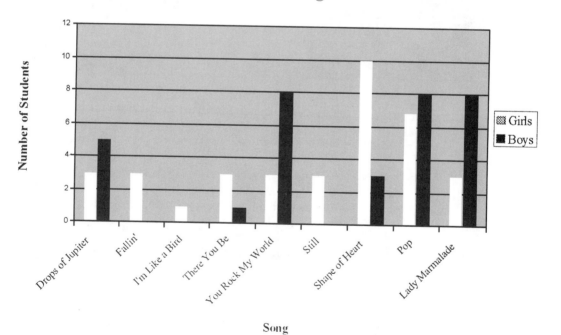

FIGURE 11.3   Bar Graph Showing Music Preference Data

STUDENT ACTIVITIES

1. Select one of the sample service-learning projects in this chapter and list the social, academic, and community benefits of the project.

2. Brainstorm a list of at least ten needs that your school or community has that your students could fill through a service-learning project.

3. From your list of school or community needs, select the ones that tie directly into academic goals that your students are working on.

4. From the results of activities 2 and 3 above, design a service-learning project for your students that incorporates technology, an academic goal, and a service that could be provided to the school or community.

REFERENCES

Billig, S. (2000). Research on K–12 school-based service-learning. *Phi Delta Kappan, 81*(9), 658–664.

Hart, T. (2001). Service-learning project. Unpublished assignment for SPED 346C, California State University, Chico, CA.

Jennings, M. (2001). Two very special service-learning projects. *Phi Delta Kappan, 82*(6), 474–475.

Muscott, H. (2000). A review and analysis of a service-learning program involving students with emotional/behavioral disorders. *Education and Treatment of Children,* 23(3), 346–368.

National Service-Learning Cooperative (1998). *Essential elements of service learning.* St. Paul, MN: National Youth Leadership Council.

Sigmon, R. (1994). Serving to learn, learning to serve. *Linking service with learning.* Chicago: National Institute on Learning and Service.

- - - - -

CHAPTER TWELVE

ACCESS

Although the variety of ways that technology can improve educational, social, and vocational outcomes for students with special needs is demonstrated by the case studies and examples in this book, students, teachers, and parents encounter barriers to using technology. In this chapter, we examine the opportunities and the barriers from the perspective of policy, training, collaboration, and resources. Knowing how to use technology tools doesn't help if the tools are not available in schools, at home, and in the community. Having technology tools is not beneficial if personnel are not trained in their use, continually updated with skill development, and provided with technical support for their maintenance. Providing appropriate access to technology for students with special needs is a daunting task, and one that cannot be done without a collaborative approach, because no single entity has sufficient resources or expertise to do the job in isolation.

CHAPTER GOALS

By the end of this chapter, you will be able to:

1. list provisions of federal legislation that support access to technology for your students;
2. develop a process for your school or district to address technology needs within the IEP;
3. work collaboratively to establish a technology team to meet the technology needs of students in your school or district, with or without disabilities;
4. identify resources for assessing student needs for assistive technology;
5. identify sources of support within the community to make sure technology needs are addressed.

LEGISLATION AND POLICY

Support for students with disabilities through assistive devices has a long legislative and educational policy history, which continues in the implementation of the PL 105-17 Individuals with Disabilities Education Act (IDEA) (1997) and PL 105-394 The Assistive Technology Act (1998). IDEA mandates that every IEP team "consider assistive technology when planning for the individualized educational needs of an individual with a disability. The Assistive Technology Act extends funding of the 1988 Tech Act to assist states in promoting awareness about assistive technology and to provide technical assistance, outreach, and foster inter-agency coordination. A list of Technology Projects is included in Appendix A.

Recently introduced legislation and policy, the "New Freedom Initiative" (2001), is composed of two key components:

1. *Federal Investment in Assistive Technology Research and Development.* The Admin-istration will provide a major increase in the Rehabilitative Engineering Research Centers' budget for assistive technologies, create a new fund to help bring assistive technologies to market, and better coordinate the federal effort in prioritizing immedi-ate assistive and universally designed technology needs in the disability community.

2. *Access to Assistive Technology.* Assistive technology is often prohibitively expen-sive. In order to increase access, funding for low-interest loan programs to purchase assistive technologies will increase significantly.

Both are intended to increase access to assistive and universally designed technologies. Many teachers, parents, and service providers have not yet begun to integrate assistive technology assessment and services into their program planning, except for those students with physical or communication disabilities. However,

> IDEA requires that assistive technology must be considered for each student for whom an Individualized Education Program is developed. This requirement clearly places greater emphasis on assistive technology for students with disabilities than was the case prior to the enactment of that legislation. School personnel are now required to develop policies and procedures for meeting this provision of the law (Blackhurst & Edyburn, 2000, p. 25).

Definitions of the terms *assistive technology* and *assistive technology service* from IDEA are helpful in understanding the intent of legislation and policy.

> As used in this part [§300.5], **assistive technology device** means any item, piece of equip-ment, or product system, whether acquired commercially off the shelf, modified, or custom-ized, that is used to increase, maintain, or improve the functional capabilities of a child with a disability. (Authority: 20 U.S.C. 1401(1))

FIGURE 12.1 Each student's technology needs must be assessed and addressed in the IEP.

As used in this part [§300.6], **assistive technology service** means any service that directly assists a child with a disability in the selection, acquisition, or use of an assistive technology device.

The term includes—

(a) The evaluation of the needs of a child with a disability, including a functional evaluation of the child in the child's customary environment;

(b) Purchasing, leasing, or otherwise providing for the acquisition of assistive technology devices by children with disabilities;

(c) Selecting, designing, fitting, customizing, adapting, applying, maintaining, repairing, or replacing assistive technology devices;

(d) Coordinating and using other therapies, interventions, or services with assistive technology devices, such as those associated with existing education and rehabilitation plans and programs;

(e) Training or technical assistance for a child with a disability or, if appropriate, that child's family; and

(f) Training or technical assistance for professionals (including individuals providing education or rehabilitation services), employers, or other individuals who provide services to, employ, or are otherwise substantially involved in the major life functions of that child. (Authority: 20 U.S.C. 1401(2))

THE INDIVIDUALIZED EDUCATION PROGRAM (IEP)

Whether or not the consideration of assistive technology needs for a student results in a substantive change in IEP procedure remains to be seen; the regulations are new and much remains to be done before students can be assured that their needs will be addressed appropriately.

> The least helpful type of documentation would be the use of a check-box or pre-printed statement on the IEP indicating that assistive technology has been considered and, if needed, the devices and services are specified elsewhere. This type of documentation is simply not sufficient to describe the breadth or depth of consideration that should occur and, even worse, may encourage superficial consideration of assistive technology needs (Golden, 1998, p. 13).

One framework that has been used widely by many IEP teams is the SETT organizational tool (Zabala, 1995). It considers the Student, the Environment, the Tasks required for active participation in the activities of the environment, and the Tools needed for the student to address the tasks. The questions provide team members with a means of systematically examining each student's technology needs in an individualized, qualitative, and substantive manner. Table 12.1 below outlines the SETT framework.

ASSESSMENT

Regardless of the type of disability, "the best assessment for determining if a device will work for an individual is the actual use of the device, in a natural environment, to perform the activities desired. Careful documentation of the degree to which the device provides the desired outcomes provides almost irrefutable justification for the device recommendation"

TABLE 12.1   A Brief Introduction to the SETT Framework.

The SETT Framework is an organizational tool to help collaborative teams create Student-centered, Environmentally-useful, and Tasks-focused Tool systems that foster the educational success of students with disabilities. The SETT Framework is built on the premise that in order to develop an appropriate system of assistive technology devices and services, teams must first gather information about the student, the customary environments in which the students spend their time, and the tasks that are required for the students to be active participants in the teaching/learning processes that lead to educational success. It is believed that the elements of the SETT Framework, with minor adjustments, can also be applied to non-educational environments and service plans.

Critical Elements of SETT
- Collaboration
- Communication
- Multiple Perspectives
- Pertinent information
- Shared Knowledge
- Flexibility
- On-going Processes

It must be remembered that SETT is a framework, not a protocol. The questions under each section of the SETT Framework are expected to guide discussion rather than be complete and comprehensive in and of themselves. As each of these questions is explored, it is likely that many other questions will arise. The team continues the exploration until there is consensus that there is enough shared knowledge to make an informed, reasonable decision that can be supported by data.

The Student

- What is the functional area(s) of concern? *What does the student need to be able to do that is difficult or impossible to do independently at this time?*
- Special needs (related to area of concern)
- Current abilities (related to area of concern)

The Environments

- Arrangement (instructional, physical)
- Support (available to both the student and the staff)
- Materials and Equipment (commonly used by others in the environments)
- Access Issues (technological, physical, instructional)
- Attitudes and Expectations (staff, family, others)

The Tasks

- What tasks occur in the student's natural environments that enable progress toward mastery of IEP goals and objectives?
- What tasks are required for active involvement in identified environments? (related to communication, instruction, participation, productivity, environmental control)

(continued)

TABLE 12.1 *Continued*

> ### The Tools
>
> In the SETT Framework, Tools include devices, services and strategies... everything that is needed to help the student succeed.
>
> Analyze the information gather on the Student, the Environments, and the Tasks to address the following questions and activities.
>
> - Is it expected that the student will not be able to make reasonable progress toward educational goals without assistive technology devices and services?
> - If yes, describe what a useful system of assistive technology devices and services for the student would be like.
> - Brainstorm Tools that could be included in a system that addresses student needs.
> - Select the most promising Tools for trials in the natural environments.
> - Plan the specifics of the trial (expected changes, when/how tools will be used, cues, etc.)
> - Collect data on effectiveness.
>
> It is expected that the SETT Framework will be useful during all phases of assistive technology service delivery. With that in mind, it is important to revisit the SETT Framework information periodically to determine if the information that is guiding decision-making and implementation is accurate, up to date, and clearly reflects the shared knowledge of all involved.

Source: Personal communication, March 2002. Joy Zabala, M.Ed., ATP. Contact by e-mail joy@jozabala.com.

(Golden, 2000, p. 29). For particular aspects of an assessment of technology, specialized expertise from a speech/language clinician, a physical or occupational therapist, or rehabilitation engineer may be desirable. If no one in the school or district has expertise in assistive technology assessment, the district must retain individuals with the knowledge necessary to provide this information.

Assistive technology assessment occurs at many points in the IEP process. At the screening stage, assistive technology the student is currently using may be noted, and ideas for ways the student might benefit from assistive technology may be generated.

As a part of the comprehensive evaluation for eligibility and for program planning, assistive technology evaluation might focus on academic areas, with and without assistive technology. For example, are the student's writing skills improved using a mind-map tool? A talking word processor? A spell checker? Can the student maintain focus on a task more effectively with pencil and paper or using a computer? Specific aspects of assistive technology evaluation are also addressed within the disability-specific chapter of this book.

The evaluation of a student's assistive technology needs can also be done as a separate part of the evaluation. These separate considerations may be appropriate when the student's needs are very specific, such as hearing aids or the specifications of a magnification system for a student with visual impairment, for example.

Ideally, assistive technology assessment is integrated within the comprehensive evaluation and focuses on using the technology within the types of tasks the student is actually required to do as a part of his or her educational program. Looking at the student's performance in a natural setting (rather than the artificial assessment setting) is the best way to judge the impact the assistive technology will have on the student's performance.

Districts are fearful of the costs of providing assistive technology, and they are also wary of expensive mistakes, such as getting a tool that a student doesn't use enough to justify the expense. The SETT framework sets up a system in which a continuum of options are reviewed, some no- or low-tech and depending on the situation, some high-tech. The key is the "consideration" that each child's needs receive. Beigel (2000) cautions IEP team members to "put the individual user of AT at the center of the assessment process" (p. 237), rather than going for "gee-whiz" technology that doesn't live up to expectations for its use. Table 12.2 provides useful questions in addition to those provided in the SETT framework (Table 12.1).

TABLE 12.2   Questions for the AT Assessment

LEARNER CHARACTERISTICS	SCHOOL CHARACTERISTICS	DEVICE CHARACTERISTICS
What purposeful motoric movement does the learner have?	How do teachers of learners using assistive technology present information to the learners?	How durable is the device?
How willing is the learner to try new activities or tasks?	What is the preferred learning–teaching interaction style of the classroom—a cooperative style, an individualized style, project-driven, or small independent and dependent groups?	What is the willingness of the vendor of the device to provide a trial or loaner period of use for the learner?
What does the learner desire from the use of assistive technology?	What is the primary method of assessment in the classroom?	What is the general reputation of the company in terms of construction, service, training, and reliability?
What supports will the learner require in using the device?	How receptive is the teacher to having a learner who uses assistive technology in the classroom?	Does the learner have the psychomotor skills needed to use the device in a functional manner where benefit is gained, or merely on an operational level where the learner can turn the device on and off?
What impact will the learner's socioeconomic status and cultural background have on the use of AT?	What is the physical structure of the classroom and school? Is the school spacious enough for learners with mobility needs?	Is the device aesthetically acceptable to the learner?
What levels of training will the learner and others who interact with the learner need?		Will the device meet the needs of the individual in the school environment in a manner that is transparent or easily understood by those who interact with the learner?
		How portable is the device?
		How easy is the device to update and repair?

From "Assistive Technology Assessment: More than the Device" by A. Beigel, 2000, *Intervention in School and Clinic, 35,* 237–243. Copyright 2000 by PRO-ED, Inc. Reprinted with permission.

TECHNOLOGY TO ENHANCE THE OVERALL
ASSESSMENT PROCESS

Consideration of a student's need for technology is an important aspect of the assessment process. A second aspect of technology in the assessment process is how technology can be used to gather, organize, store, and present information on the student's needs, accomplishments, and work samples.

Informal Assessment

For example, teachers can use the PalmPilot™ and special software to collect behavioral data (anecdotes, tallies of on- and off-task behavior, etc.). The data can then be downloaded to a computer where it can analyzed and graphed.

Teachers can use one of the many Internet sites to generate quick assessments and worksheets to pinpoint skill strengths and weaknesses (e.g., *www.quia.com* [matching games, flash cards], *www.discovery.com* [crossword puzzle generators].) Using a game-like format may ease the stress of pressure of a testing situation and enable a student to do his or her best.

Curriculum-Based Assessment

Curriculum-based assessment is characterized by frequent collection of student performance data that are typical of classroom curricula with frequent, specific feedback to students and parents. Many software programs come with built-in assessments of skills such as reading comprehension or math computational skills (Accelerated Reader, Accelerated Math, Quick Flash, etc.).

Three reading assessment programs include: Online Reader (EBSCO), for students in grades 4–12, available in both Web-based and CD versions; Accelerated Reader (Advantage Learning Systems), and Reading Counts (Scholastic) for grades K–12. These tools provide reading selections and tests to assess and improve reading comprehension skills. They also provide ways to monitor individual progress, and teachers and students get reports on student progress.

Standardized Assessment

A wide range of software programs are available that have one or more of the following capabilities in regard to a particular standardized test, such as the Woodcock-Johnson Achievement Test, the STAR tests of academic skills, the Peabody Individual Achievement Test, and so on:

1. diagnostic programs
2. interpretation of test results
3. information management of test results and data
4. report writing
5. generation of instructional strategies, goals, and objectives

In addition to the possibilities of computerized assessment and computation of scores, teachers and service providers can use their word processors to save sample paragraphs for reports and summaries, improving productivity immeasurably. Sample paragraphs saved under different descriptive titles can be edited and merged into an individualized report.

Electronic Portfolios

As schools move toward more performance-based and authentic assessment approaches and toward instruction based on multiple intelligences, both low-tech and electronic portfolios are required for some grades statewide. Just what is an electronic portfolio, and what information does it add to our knowledge and understanding about what students can and cannot do? An electronic portfolio is a student folder that includes a selection of work produced over time and the student's evaluation of the contents (Johnson, 1994).

Gardner's vision of classrooms of the future (1991) features student-created multimedia exhibits to demonstrate their understanding of different curricular topics. Students create multimedia book reports, biographies, math story problems, and science projects, and store their "works" on audiotapes, videotapes, computer disks, CD's and on Web sites. Each student gets the opportunity to show his or her work in a public exhibition on a rotating, periodic basis (D'Ignazio, 1994), or they can maintain their portfolios on the school or class Web site, where family, friends, and community can view the students' progress.

Integrated software tools with word processing, database, spreadsheets, and presentation software are commonly used in portfolios (such as Microsoft Office™, Claris-Works™, or AppleWorks™), in which students express their ideas graphically and in pictures, tables, and charts. Students can include explanations of their thinking in writing or in their own recorded voices or QuickTime™ movies.

At Van Cortlandt Middle School in New York, all eighth-grade students were required to create a multimedia portfolio including documents, images, video, and audio clips (Milone, 1995). All students were expected to show competence in five areas: aesthetics, problem solving, research, and out-of-class activities, such as hobbies and volunteer work. At the end of the year, these areas serve as the basis by which a panel of parents, teachers, and peers evaluate the portfolios. The portfolios are also presented at an open house at the school and are transferred to video for parents to take home.

One teacher reported, "Many of the students who were doing average or below average work produced remarkable portfolios. We discovered that we could not predict who could create the best portfolios. The process of creating an opening screen, choosing work to be included, and actually creating the portfolio empowered students and made them feel more responsible for their work" (Milone, 1995, p. 29).

At Gateway School in Santa Cruz, California, all sixth graders did presentations of their written country reports using PowerPoint. At The Foundry, an alternative school for troubled teenagers in San Jose, students created "Me-Books" to portray their lives, their hopes and aspirations, and their interests. At graduation, students prepared a speech to follow the multimedia presentation (Male, 2000).

At Horizon Community Middle School in Aurora, Colorado, students used Hyper-Studio™ for their electronic portfolios. A teacher there commented:

Many of the students who are put off by high-stakes tests are less anxious and more enthusiastic about portfolios. Some of the students who were underachieving academically found the portfolio project to be an incentive to push themselves. Students had the opportunity to present their portfolios to a large audience using either an LCD projection device or multiple television screens around the room. Students reviewed their work in collaboration with the teacher to determine if they met state-set standards in various subject areas (Milone, 1995, p. 32).

Two schools in Florida, A. D. Henderson in Boca Raton, and Ahfachkee School on a nearby Seminole reservation, used a template for Linkway Live™ called Multimedia Assessment Tool. These portfolios contained not only student work but management information as well. The home page for each student contains a picture and buttons that can be clicked to show information (when and were the student catches the bus and arrives home), a historical picture of the student's school record, attendance, and academic objectives. Samples of what students put in their portfolios included:

- Spelling: a scanned image of a student's spelling test with the student doing a voice-over reading;
- Writing: a handwritten letter with student voice-over ;
- Science: a video of the student engaged in a seed experiment, explaining what he or she is doing.

The portfolio also included video footage of a student–teacher conference (Milone, 1995, p. 36).

Hanfland (1999) reports on a districtwide implementation of electronic portfolios using HyperStudio™. The teachers used a template on which each student recorded personal information about themselves, examples of their best work, school activities, and goals for the year. Each area has a link to another card that stores detailed information for viewing. Each student's portfolio was stored on a floppy disk (with the growing ease of burning CDs, there is not much difference in cost, and CDs may be accessible to more computers). Hanfland found that the electronic portfolios

motivate students to produce quality work, and they also increase students' self-esteem by showcasing their best work. Portfolios provide methodical flexibility, allow for various learning styles, increase students' retention of content, increase student responsibility, and help develop their computer literacy skills (p. 57). IBM's Learning Village Web-based portfolio offers schools and districts a flexible way to store teacher and student portfolios.

SPECIFYING TECHNOLOGY AS A SERVICE IN THE IEP

Because the IEP is considered a legal contract to provide services, parents and IEP team members may want to assure that adequate support is available to the student to use the technology the team believes is essential to the student's educational program. Table 12.3 provides some examples of statements from IEPs for different disabilities (Golden, 1997, p. 16).

TABLE 12.3 Sample Statement from IEPs

SERVICE	FREQUENCY	BEGIN	END	LOCATION
Visual impairment: Special instruction in using scanning/ screen reader	50 min/wk	9/1/01	5/20/02	regular classroom
Multiple disabilities: Speech/ language therapy assistance with voice output augmentative communication system	60 min/wk	9/6/01	9/6/01	All educational settings and home
Hearing impairment: Speech therapy and audiology assistance with amplication system and captioning access		9/1/01	6/15/02	Regular classroom and speech resource room

WRITING GOALS AND OBJECTIVES

Goals are broad, general statements of direction and categories of skills that can be used as guidelines for designing more specific instructional objectives and learning activities. Objectives may or may not include a specific piece of software. Some parents and teachers feel that specifying the software may be important; others worry that specifying software may work against the student's ability to transfer the needed skill to situations when technology is not available, or that the student might be limited to a particular piece of software when an improved program becomes available. One way of balancing these two opinions is to specify software when appropriate and also include specific objectives for transferring the skill to other, nontechnology situations.

Examples of goals and objectives are provided in Table 12.4.

TEAMWORK, PARTNERSHIPS, AND COLLABORATION

Given a scarcity of resources, effective collaboration will increase access to technology for all students. One way of building in collaboration regarding technology resources is to establish a school technology team, part of whose responsibility is to assure access to assistive technology for students with special needs. Some of the individuals who can assist with assessments for AT include the following:

- A general education teacher who can help the team identify what AT would be helpful to students with disabilities who are spending all or part of their time in the general education classroom;
- Parents (and students) who can show how AT is being used at home and under what circumstances it could be used at school;
- A speech/language pathologist who can assess the student's communication needs and determine what technology could help improve the student's interactions with others;

TABLE 12.4   Examples of Goals and Objectives with Technology in the IEP

CURRICULUM	GOAL	OBJECTIVE
Social studies	To participate in class discussions and oral presentations	Using a programmed electronic device, Sara will present an oral report that meets the standard for the country report with a rubric score of 3 or better.
Social skills	To make friends	Using an electronic communication device, Sam will respond appropriately to social inquiries from classmates 5 times out of 5 opportunities over two consecutive days.
Language arts/reading	To complete written work as assigned	Susan will use a computer and printer to complete all reading comprehension exercises that other students do with pencil and paper.
Language arts	To write an essay	Using a word-processing program with a spell checker, Tom will compose a three-paragraph paper composed of 15 or more sentences with a minimum of 80% accuracy in the use of spelling, punctuation, and grammar in five trials.

From *Assistive Technology Assessment in Special Education: Policy and Practice* by D. Golden, CASE/TAM Assistive Technology Policy and Practice Group, 1998, p. 16. Reprinted with permission of Council of Administrators of Special Education.

■ A physical therapist and an occupational therapist who determine what skills are needed to use the AT devices and how to position the student to obtain the best function;
■ The school's computer coordinator or a teacher who can help determine which hardware and software may be available in the district and how it can be modified; they also might be able to help procure the equipment and train the students and staff to use it;
■ An assistive technology specialist (ATS) if the district is fortunate to have such a person on staff or has contracted for the services of one.

SUCCESSFUL TECHNOLOGY TEAM MODELS

In Lawrence, New York, a "Pathways Team" was formed at each school, composed of teachers from several consecutive grade levels, the administrator, and support personnel, such as the resource teacher. The teams met to develop curriculum activities to support the integration of students with disabilities using a variety of technologies. Periodically, the teams from all the school sites would meet to share progress with particular students, ideas for curriculum adaptations, and explore new technologies (Moeller, Jeffers, Zorfass, & Capel, 1995). The role of facilitator on the team was considered of such importance that two facilitators were used: one to train teachers and one to secure resources (funding, equipment, software) and arrange for professional development time, select consultants to help with implementation, schedule activities, and conduct ongoing evaluations of progress.

School districts with Alliance for Technology Access centers nearby (see Appendix A for a list of centers) have taken advantage of the centers' expertise and range of equipment and software to meet the needs of their students. The CITE center in Orlando, Florida, for example, offers a summer computer camp at which a wide array of communication devices and switches are available to try out. Parents can observe their child's success with a variety of equipment and software and share ideas with school personnel when the IEP team meets to plan the next year's program. Based on the team's recommendations, appropriate equipment and software can be purchased.

Laren Scrivo, eight years old, from Fairfield, New Jersey, had a successful experience at a technology center. She and her family worked with the Center for Enabling Technology in Whippany, New Jersey, where they discovered Ke:nx software and a trackball for easier movement of the cursor. An adaptive keyboard, the Magic Wand, provided a more appropriate input system, and using Co:Writer (word prediction), Lauren was able to work much more quickly. CET worked with her parents and school to purchase these new tools and a classroom computer. The school also made architectural changes to make the school more accessible. "Everyone at the school—from the principal on down—has embraced the concept of full inclusion and is committed to making Lauren's experience a success," reported her mother. "We have nothing but praise for their efforts" (Alliance for Technology Access, 1995, p. 31).

FUNDING

Districts are fearful of bringing technology into the schools because of the added expense such tools may entail. Assistive technology can range from no cost/low cost items to those of considerable expense. If an IEP team determines that a particular AT device or service is needed for a student's free appropriate public education, then it is the responsibility of the district to provide the device.

A more effective way of addressing the issue would be for districts to investigate funding options before the need arises. Using teamwork and a proactive approach will build credibility with parents and community and result in more access to technology for students. Districts will discover that a solution will require a combination of funds from a variety of sources for the purchase of assistive technology. A successful plan includes coordinating efforts, seeking multiple funding sources, researching information on how the organization makes funding decisions, and locating information on who makes funding decisions within the organization. The bottom line is that, without alternative funding sources, the school district remains responsible for providing AT devices required for students to benefit from their education.

Depending on the ages and needs of students and the specific circumstances, some funding source alternatives might include, but are not limited to, private insurance (with parental permission), Medicaid, Vocational Rehabilitation, Supplemental Security Income (SSI), Early Periodic Screening Diagnostic Testing (EPSDT), Plan to Achieve Self-Support (PASS), or special foundations and civic organizations such as the Make-a-Wish Foundation of America, United Cerebral Palsy of America, Easter Seals, Elks, Lions, Kiwanis, Shriners, Rotary, and Optimists. In some cases, the family will choose to purchase the device, but they cannot be coerced to do so. Research shows that funding remains the single greatest barrier to the acquisition of assistive technology. The best response to this dilemma is a creative and innovative cooperative approach (Brennan, 1998).

STUDENT ACTIVITIES

1. Describe your school or school district's policies and procedures related to assistive technology. What policies or procedures could be improved? What policies or procedures are you proud of?

2. What process does your school or school district use to assist parents in getting funding for assistive technology? How could this process be improved to provide greater support for students and their families?

3. Review the IEPs of three students in your program whose educational program would be enhanced with assistive technology. Are their technology needs addressed in the IEP? If yes, how? If no, why not?

4. Make a database of assistive devices available in your school or district. Include a description of the device, the source of funding, the location/current user of the device, and situations in which the device might be appropriate. Disseminate the database to those who would benefit from the data.

REFERENCES

Alliance for Technology Access. (1995). Real people, real technology, real solutions. *Exceptional Parent,* 25(11), 30–31, 32, 34.

Assistive Technology Act (1998). Washington, DC: US Government Printing Office.

Beigel, A. (2000). Assistive technology assessment: More than the device. *Intervention in School and Clinic, 35*(4), 237–43.

Blackhurst, A. E., & Edyburn, D. (2000). A brief history of special education technology. *Special Education Technology Practice, 2*(1), 21–36.

Brennan, J. (1998). Assistive technology: It takes a team. *The Delta Kappa Gamma Bulletin. 64*(2), 24–28.

Chambers, A. C. (1997). Has technology been considered: A guide for IEP teams. Reston, VA: CASE/TAM of the Council for Exceptional Children.

D'Ignazio, F. (1994). The classroom as knowledge theme park. *The Computing Teacher, 21*(7), 35–37.

Gardner, H. (1991). *UnSchooled minds: How children think.* New York: Basic Books.

Golden, D. (1998). *Assistive technology in special education: Policy and practice.* Albuquerque, NM: Council of Special Education Administrators/Technology and Media Division of the Council for Exceptional Children.

Hanfland, P. (1999). Electronic portfolios: Students documenting their best work. *Learning and Leading with Technology, 26*(6), 54–57.

Individuals with Disabilities Education Act (1997 amendments). Washington, DC: US Government Printing Office.

Johnson, J. (1994). Portfolio assessment in mathematics: Lessons from the field. *The Computing Teacher, 21*(6), 22–23.

Male, M. (2000). *Strategies for learning: Creating exemplary alternative education programs for ALL students.* A presentation for the Teacher Education Division, Council for Exceptional Children, Las Vegas, NV.

Milone, M. (1995). Electronic portfolios: Who's doing them and how? *Technology & Learning, 16*(2), 28–36.

Moeller, B., Jeffers, L., Zorfass, J., & Capel, H. (1995). Forging special pathways. *Electronic Learning, 15*(3), 18–19.

Zabala, J. (1995). The SETT framework: Critical areas to consider when making informed assistive technology decisions. ERIC: ED 381962.

CHAPTER THIRTEEN

CREATING A VISION OF TECHNOLOGY FOR EMPOWERMENT

Alan Kay, one of the pioneers in the development of the personal computer, has noted that, until technology becomes as accessible as pencil and paper, we cannot expect technology to revolutionize the way students learn. Can you imagine telling students that their turn to use the pencil and paper will be a 30-minute period next Thursday? As Skip Via says:

> We can no longer be content to operate one-computer classrooms and think that we are participants in the Information Revolution. That's like having one glove for a baseball team or one textbook for a classroom. If we want students to learn the kind of skills that the business world already requires of them, then we had better be able to provide them with the necessary tools. How much technology is enough? When we think of computers as pencils, rather than as subjects, we will have begun to reach that point (1991, p. 6).

This chapter will present snapshots of classrooms and communities that have been successful in using technology (along with the best of everything else we know about effective instruction) to enable all students to succeed. Just as important, however, is the impact of technology on teachers, family, and communities. Using the philosophy of "It takes a village," this chapter will explore the impact of a shared vision in community and schools in reaping the benefits of technology for students. You will be encouraged to question the way things have always been.

CHAPTER GOALS

When you finish this chapter, you will have:

1. reflected on your own vision of your students' special needs and how technology might be used to increase the quality of their educational experience;
2. created a vision of your classroom, school, and community, reflecting on:
   - making diversity a strength
   - emphasizing learning strategies and processes, not just right answers

- putting students at the center of educational planning
- creating opportunities for maximum social and cognitive development within supportive environments
- valuing the role of teacher and learner for all participants (teachers, students, and families);

3. shared your vision with colleagues and community to determine the level of support for student-centered, curriculum-rich learning at your school and in your community.

A VISION IN FOCUS

Creating a vision does not mean waiting until all the elements are in place before the work begins. Regardless of the degree of inclusiveness of the setting in which you and your students now work, and regardless of the amount of technological resources currently available, the first step in the process of creating an exceptional classroom, school, or community is to have a clear vision that can be achieved in incremental steps.

In the groundbreaking work of the Apple Classrooms of Tomorrow (ACOT), the most significant feature of the successful projects was "a common vision of where you want to be" (Gooden, 1996, p. 157). The ACOT vision of "environments where technologies were used as knowledge-building tools for communication and collaboration, media-rich composition, and simulation and modeling across the curriculum" (Sandholtz, Ringstaff, & Dwyer, 1997, p. 10) contrasted sharply with traditional approaches to teaching. Over the ten-year period of research on the impact of technology on teachers and learners, the shared vision produced:

- highly motivated students and teachers
- greater time spent on assignments and focused on academic learning (on-task behavior)
- increases in student initiative (students went beyond basic requirements of assignments and explored new applications and skills on their own)
- students took more risks and and were less concerned about making mistakes; they exhibited less fear of failure (Sandholtz, Ringstaff, & Dwyer, 1996).

Technology presents us with a tool like none we've had before, and challenges our thinking about teaching and learning, abilities and disabilities, and the boundaries of our world. What is possible is limited only by our own imagination or vision. As one ACOT teacher put it:

> As you work into using the computer in the classroom, you start questioning everything you have done in the past and wonder how you can adapt it to the computer. Then you start questioning the whole concept of what you originally did (Sandholtz et al., 1997, p. 17).

STUDENT EMPOWERMENT

> Once you have learned how to ask relevant and appropriate questions, you have learned how to learn and no one can keep you from learning whatever you want or need to know (Postman & Weingartner, 1969, p. 6).

Via describes the success he experienced in incorporating extensive use of technology into his inclusive classroom:

> Students and teachers are using technology to work directly with source materials and to explore areas of interest within the regular curriculum. They are learning to research and gather information from a variety of sources, synthesize it, and create original reports and presentations. They control the technology for their own purposes rather than being controlled by it for purposes established by software houses. Can you imagine a better way to integrate special students into 'regular' settings? When students can work at their own pace, there is no 'norm'. Each individual can work to his or her potential and contribute to others' learning. And there can be expanded flexibility to include specialists or therapists in small groups. A classroom can be a resource room for everyone (1991, pp. 6–7).

Examples of empowerment abound in the teachers' logs from the ACOT classrooms (Sandholtz et al., 1997):

> Teachers saw less advanced students blossom, unpopular students gain peer approval, and unmotivated students stay in to work at recess:

>> Jose is the talkative, annoying misfit kind of kid which every teacher has had at some time. He loves the computer. He has not been popular with his peers, but he has caught on very quickly to the programming language. Other students are asking, 'Can Jose come over and help me?' It is interesting to see how becoming an expert has influenced his class relationships.
>>
>> In some cases, particular computer projects sparked students' interest and tapped a hidden skill. Two high school students 'who are noted as low achievers by everyone, including the students,' got turned on by a robotics project and 'worked seriously all the time.' Fourth grade students 'who do not usually receive as much recognition as others have proven to be very good at solving problems when staging original stories as a play using the software program.' A first-grade student 'who is low to average on academics is a whiz at word processing and finished all 21 lessons of that program today.' In a fourth-grade classroom, a student 'who doesn't do well in many courses is a whiz at patterns, and he was the only one to figure out the puzzle.'

When the curriculum is transformed by access to technology, students themselves experience transformation. For example, at St. Benedict's Preparatory School in Newark, teachers developed an interdisciplinary course called Newark Studies, in which students focus on issues in the community (pollution, crime, disease) and use simulation software to design their own cities, coming to grips with how complex problems in the community are. The culmination of the class is the publication of Newark InDepth, a magazine sold and distributed to Newark residents (Gooden, 1996).

At Canyon Middle School in Castro Valley, California, Joyce Burtch agreed to include three students with moderate neurological and physical impairments in her Internet telecommunications class for seventh graders. Nicole, Cahani, and Carl E-mailed keypals who had special learning needs in Milford, New Jersey, every other day. Their E-mails included descriptions of daily activities and included photos as well as questions about their keypals' interests and activities. The students in Milford's Holland Township school were equally engaged in the activity; their progress resulted in their school achieving "Star

School Status" for technology, the only elementary school in New Jersey to be recognized that year. Following seven weeks of E-mail exchanges, students published books of their correspondence, which they practiced reading (Burtch, 1999).

TEACHER EMPOWERMENT

Concetta Petrone, science department head at South Philadelphia High, discovered an abandoned greenhouse among an accumulation of cast-off items. This discovery led her to propose a project to promote hands-on activities in botany, using computers as learning tools for urban students with extremely limited opportunities in the science of botany or anything related to plant life. Her project paired students of varying abilities to cultivate their own plants using computers to record growth data, conduct planned growth simulations, and write detailed reports on everything from photosynthesis to acid rain. This project was so successful that community support poured in from garden supply businesses, horticulturists, and even a senior center, whose participants helped plant trees in a weedpatch on the school grounds.

The success of this project led to a follow-up project to monitor the water quality of a local tributary for the Delaware Riverkeeper Network. Another project led students to help residents identify energy savings resulting from insulating, using computer simulations. Students' high level of motivation, achievement, and initiative led other teachers to integrate computer technology and multimedia tools in other subjects (Gooden, 1996).

Teachers in Dos Palos, California, launched a "Career Path" project to prepare students for life beyond the dwindling job prospects of the small community. Several initiatives quadrupled the number of students qualified for college, even as risk factors for the same population doubled. A project using computers to reinforce links between academics and vocational training provided students with "lifetime warranties" that certified their preparation for the world of work. Computers are used in virtually every area of the high school curriculum from graphic arts and drafting to journalism and agriculture. Two students took the initiative to produce a Spanish version of the school newspaper (Gooden, 1996).

The teachers at Willow Bend School in Illinois used technology as a catalyst to completely redesign teaching and learning at the school (Conyers, Kappel, & Rooney, 1999). The philosophy they adopted was, "We use technology to learn, not just learn to use technology." Teachers who were uncomfortable with this vision were given the opportunity to transfer. Following a year of staff development and planning, the transformed school opened with a new curriculum, instructional approaches, assessment processes, and technology. Students were grouped in multi-age settings. Round tables replaced desks; folding doors replaced walls to encourage team teaching. Children entered the building as soon as they arrived at school. Teachers met weekly in teams, and some chose to team teach. Teachers and students formed two K–6 academies to benefit from a small school environment.

Science and social studies are taught in thematic units taught each afternoon on a two-year rotation. Distance learning activities are included so that students work with peers from around the world to look for solutions to local, national, and international problems. In an oceanography unit, for example, students E-mail the captain and crew of a ship sailing around the world. Staff chose software such as WiggleWorks™, a 72-book library on a CD-ROM with interactive tools to support reading, writing, speaking, and listening, built on universal design principles. Telephones in each classroom connect school, home, and community. Students collect their work in an electronic portfolio that is saved on a CD-ROM at the end of the year to record their progress through each year at Willow Bend.

Willow Bend's test scores have risen significantly to a level well above district averages and state performance standards. Attendance is higher at this school than at any other in the district. Awards for performance are numerous.

FAMILY EMPOWERMENT

Parents have visions and dreams for their child that may be expressed differently from a school's vision, but they must be considered just as important and included in educational planning, if a team approach is to be successful.

> For many professionals, it is scary to hear a family's dreams because they seem 'unrealistic.' Professionals feel inadequate to deal with these dreams because they are not sure that they can make the family's dreams come true. However, even if the dreams seem 'unrealistic,' it is important for professionals to respect and validate the family's dreams (Sloand-Armstrong & Jones, 1995, p. 2).

When teachers, families and students work together toward a common vision, amazing things happen. One example is Victor, whose experience is related in *Computer Resources for People with Disabilities* (Alliance for Technology Access, 1996, p. 8):

> Victor had a vision. To him it was simple: go to school with his peers, graduate from high school with a New York State Regents' diploma, go to college, get a job, and live independently. Victor had cerebral palsy and was nonverbal. He advocated for the development of his own technology support team, which included a rehabilitation counselor, a technology resource person, a high school counselor, and a tutor. Victor was empowered by his vision far more than the technology. He expected that the technology was there or would be developed.

SCHOOL/COMMUNITY EMPOWERMENT

In Abita Springs, Louisiana, a multicultural focus of the social studies curriculum led the teachers to design projects in which students collect and write stories, develop presentations, and create a CD-ROM encyclopedia of the folklore of the region. No longer are students limited by the material in their textbook; students see themselves as creators of curriculum and can identify their significance in history, bringing their studies to real life and connecting their learning in meaningful ways to their community (Gooden, 1996).

Students on the Pine Ridge reservation in South Dakota explored Native American myths and legends and have connected their work to similar efforts on other reservations across the country. Students used multimedia to present their work and created a CD-ROM to share with others. Students who had not been successful academically in the past found strengths that were tapped by this project, which recognized creativity, initiative, artistic design, and knowledge of customs and history of the area.

ELEMENTS OF A VISION: FOCUSING ON THE RESULTS—WHAT IS SUCCESS?

What, exactly, is a vision, and how does having a vision affect a teacher's day-to-day life with students? A vision is a consciously created fantasy of what we would ideally like to happen. A vision is not handed down from school administration; a vision must come from within each person. To develop a school- or communitywide vision, all participants must spend time together in a process of imagining what outcomes they want for students, parents, teachers, and community members. A vision is an expression of the spiritual and idealistic sides of our nature and comes from the heart, not the head. It should represent a substantial change from what exists currently, a quantum leap to making greater contributions to the lives of others. In the words of Thoreau, "If a man advances confidently in the direction of his dreams to live the life he has imagined, he will meet with a success unexpected in the common hours" (p. 214).

For teachers and service providers in special education, the emphasis on measurable goals and objectives, and focusing on short-term outcomes limits our opportunity for vision. In this book, you are encouraged to think big: Imagine how the world would be if we created opportunities for inclusion and educational success for all, with technology as a support. Here are some questions to think about:

- What would be happening for your students if you had appropriate technology to support their participation in a variety of in- and out-of-school learning opportunities?
- Who would be a part of these learning opportunities?
- What kinds of structures would be needed for learning to be optimized?
- How would you plan for the rapid changes of technology over time?
- How would the learning opportunities change over time?

The vision of one elementary school in San Jose, California, illustrates the power of technology as a tool for change:

Students experience complex, challenging real-world problem solving requiring multiple abilities of thinking, discussing, writing, and analyzing. Students learn in mixed-age and non-graded classrooms, heterogeneous groupings, peer- and cross-age tutoring programs, cooperative learning situations; retention is not needed as a means to address low achievement. Teachers seek continuous professional growth, are recognized as leaders, mentors, and educational entrepreneurs; they earn professional advancement through career ladders. Collegial support, team teaching, and opportunities for collaborating with peers on projects are built into the school structure, schedule, and calendar. Students are supported by partnerships among parents, community, education, and business to enhance career-focused learning opportunities for all students. Students use state-of-the-art equipment under the guidance of thoroughly trained teachers to support their learning outcomes with such tools as computers, CD-ROM, laserdisc players, video production equipment, telecommunications and multimedia. Student performance is measured by authentic, performance-based assessment practices that are complex and challenging (San Jose Unified School District, 1992, pp. 185–186).

PROCESS OF DEVELOPING AND SHARING A VISION
OF TECHNOLOGY FOR INCLUSION

Begin with yourself. Take the time to reflect about yourself, your students, their families, the school culture, and the community. Write down your dreams.

Find a colleague with whom to share your reflections, who is also willing to go through similar reflecting/thinking processes. Bring up your ideas with your school faculty, school site council, and your administrators. Your school or district may already be involved in strategic planning efforts. Link what you are trying to do with ongoing school restructuring, reform, and strategic planning.

Involve parents of your students in the process. The idea is to check out your visions with those of key stakeholders (other teachers, service providers, parents, community leaders) to gather support for what you want to happen.

One model of strategic planning involves the following steps (Council for Exceptional Children, 1991):

- develop a common vision (what should be)
- scan the environment (what is currently happening)
- assess the problems (the difference between what is and what should be, the barriers to and opportunities for change)
- select outcomes
- choose strategies and activities
- build support
- establish accountability/metrics to measure success

Whatever model of planning you choose, beginning with a compelling vision is the most important step. Tables 13.1 and 13.2 provide tools for brainstorming elements of your vision.

The visions written by two special educators illustrate the possibilities.

VISION 1
Students are provided with an opportunity to dream of their future and are encouraged to explore their dreams. Students are provided with a variety of technological supports to enhance their education. Students are equipped with the technology and provided an education to create a desire and a capability to explore their world. Students work in cooperative groups. Teachers are trained and educated in technology that supports student learning.

TABLE 13.1 Brainstorming Elements of a Vision

WHAT SHOULD BE	WHAT IS

TABLE 13.2   Problem/Opportunity Brainstorming

BARRIERS	OPPORTUNITIES
_____	_____
_____	_____
_____	_____

The vision I have for my students with autism at Loma Vista is to increase their accessibility to communicate, develop inclusion strategies that incorporate technology, and empower the students to advance at their own pace. Unfortunately, at the current time, there aren't technological tools to assist the students with autism in their social and learning development. Tools such as speech synthesizers, touch screen computers with picture and word icons, and CD-Rom programs to increase communication skills would encourage student-centered learning. Enabling students with autism to use accommodative devices which provides a gateway for communication would revolutionize their education experience. Technological tools would give students accessibility to language, communication skills, and interactive learning. Appropriate technology in the classroom would provide access for optimal learning and social interactions. On a personal side, the student with autism would have greater success in social and academic settings, confidence, greater peer interaction and acceptance, as well as a sense of empowerment. With proper use of technological tools, education for students and those who may interact with students, consistency, and set learning goals in place, success will be attainable for students with autism. It is important to keep updated on technological advances and how [they] can be incorporated with existing tools within the classroom. Over time, students' learning opportunities will thrive. With the support of staff, parents, and students, learning can be successful for all.

VISION 2

In my vision, qualified special educators and counselors would have enough time and resources to make a thorough assessment of the learners' needs and then supply them with whatever they need to be successful. If a student is reading too slowly, get them books on tape so they can keep ahead with their studies. (One of my high school students was cutting his watered-down special ed government class to go to a regular ed economics course. He was bored! He could have been so successful in general ed with just a little help—a tape recorder, a word processing program…). Use a mind-mapping or outlining software to help them organize their thoughts before writing. Have them E-mail assignments to the professor rather than waiting and forgetting them at home. Use speech recognition software to compensate for fine motor difficulties. Rather than dwell on the students' deficits, build on their strengths and teach them how to navigate around their disabilities to meet their goals.

The most obvious barriers to my vision are the two things needed to accomplish it: time and money. Electronic equipment and ongoing staff training is expensive. Many older students are convinced they are not intelligent and have lapsed into a permanent state of learned helplessness. They may have other financial obligations besides education, like work and family. They may be uncertain around computers and other technology. The teacher does not have much control, if any, over the students' support system. Some students with disabilities, such as those with Asperger's syndrome, prefer on-line friendships to uncomfortable face-to-face interactions. However, many students with disabilities still need help in the area of social skills and relationships.

In conclusion, I hope that technology continues to play an important role in the education of those with learning disabilities. As a teacher, I get to see firsthand the fruits of their success—increased self-esteem, a better life. When more and more people are educated, productive citizens, it benefits us all.

STUDENT ACTIVITIES

1. Use Tables 13.1 and 13.2 to think about your school's current use of technology and to imagine what might be possible. Draw a picture of the current situation and your "ideal" situation.

2. Using your notes and pictures from Activity 1, write a one- or two-page paper that describes your vision of technology and inclusion for your students. How are effective learning situations structured? In what ways are learning opportunities inclusive? In what ways is technology utilized? What adaptations are required for students to have access to technology?

3. Why is it important to have a vision when you, your school, or district sees a need to change?

REFERENCES

Alliance for Technology Access. (1996). *Computer resources for people with disabilities.* Alameda, CA: Hunter House.

Burtch, J. (1999). Technology is for everyone. *Educational Leadership, 56*(5), 33–34.

Conyers, J., Kappel, T., & Rooney, J. (1999). How technology can transform a school. *Educational Leadership, 56*(5), 82–89.

Council for Exceptional Children. (1991). *National Institute on Comprehensive System of Personnel Development Collaboration—Strategic Planning.* Reston, VA.

Gooden, A. (1996). *Computers in the classroom: How teachers and students are using technology to transform learning.* San Francisco: Jossey-Bass.

Kay, A. (1988). Personal Communication.

Postman, N., & Weingartner, C. (1969). *Teaching as a subversive activity.* New York: Delacorte Press.

Sandholtz, J., Ringstaff, C., & Dwyer, D. (1997). *Teaching with technology: Creating student-centered classrooms.* New York: Teachers College Press.

San Jose Unified School District. (1992). *Midtown Elementary Academy: A magnet technology school of tomorrow.* San Jose, CA.

Sloand-Armstrong, J., & Jones, K. (1995). Using family dreams to develop meaningful goals involving assistive technology. *Closing the Gap, 14*(2), 2, 6.

Thoreau, H. (1966). Walden. In O. Thomas (Ed.), Walden and Civil Disobedience. New York: Norton.

Via, S. (1991). How much technology is enough? *The Catalyst, 8*(3), 6–8.

■ ■ ■ ■ ■ ■

CHAPTER FOURTEEN

SCHOOLWIDE PLANNING FOR TECHNOLOGY ACCESS

Depending on the philosophy of the school, the degree of interest in implementing technology among its teachers, the leadership of the principal, the perceived needs of the students, and the resources available, school systems have opted for one or more of the following approaches:

1. *Integrated learning systems.* Students use specific computer-assisted instruction software that is usually diagnostic/prescriptive. (The students take a placement test and are placed in a set of activities based on their performance.)

2. *Computer lab.* Typically, a computer lab contains enough computers for a whole class (or half a class) to work individually. The lab may be staffed by a computer resource teacher with or without the classroom teacher of the students who are scheduled to work in the lab. The computers may be networked for printing and/or shared software. The lab's computers are usually connected to the Internet.

3. *The classroom with one computer.* The computers may be set up as stations that students can work at either in small groups or individually, depending on their assigned learning tasks.

4. *A few computers.* A learning center or library may house a few computers where students can go to do individual projects or assignments.

5. *Distance learning.* Schools are learning how to take advantage of expertise and resources at other places. Distance learning, a rapidly growing trend on university campuses, is also becoming more widely available in high schools as well.

6. *Portable labs.* Many schools are making the transition from dedicated computer labs to classroom sets of laptop or notebook computers, so that the computers can move where the students need them rather than dedicating classroom space to a computer lab. The computers may be on mobile carts so that teachers can borrow computers from each other for lessons when they would like to have all students at the computer but cannot schedule time in the computer lab.

7. *After-school learning/computer clubs.* Schools are maximizing their investment in hardware and software by offering access to technology after hours, in computer clubs or family computing events and opportunities.

Each of these approaches has strengths and limitations that will be reviewed in this chapter. Teachers will want to experiment with working in each of these settings to see which works best for particular learning tasks and curriculum, and which works best for students. Administrators, teachers, and parents should make sure whatever design the school adopts that *all* students have equitable access. Many special education teachers report that they are the last in line for equipment, software, training, or scheduled opportunities in school computer labs. Becker and Sterling (1987) report that high achieving students have the greatest access to innovative and powerful computer applications; low achievers, high risk, and students with disabilities are less likely to be in classes with these opportunities.

CHAPTER GOALS

The purpose of this chapter is to enable you to recognize the strengths and limitations of various configurations of technology within your classroom and within your school. You will be better able to participate as a knowledgeable team member as your school makes decisions about resources, facilities, and staffing related to technology access in your school. You will explore:

1. the advantages and disadvantages of computers in classrooms, labs, libraries, and integrated learning systems;
2. considerations in selecting hardware, software, and assistive devices;
3. questions to consider in planning the most effective ways to link students and teachers to technology in your school.

INTEGRATED LEARNING SYSTEMS

Integrated Learning Systems (ILS) provide a large volume of computer-based tutorials in a sequenced, integrated fashion with less need for teacher intervention. Students complete the tutorials at their own pace, and the ILS management system keeps track of student progress and presents additional remediation and enrichment activities based on assessment activities within the software (Brush, 1997).

Research on the effectiveness of ILS has been mixed. Student achievement does go up with intensive and long-term use (Wiberg, 1995). However, many teachers question the emphasis on "lock-step" approaches to learning, which make the learning process less personal and place less emphasis on affective issues (Mevarech, 1994). On the other hand, for students who have not been successful in traditional classrooms, require additional support beyond the classroom, or are in alternative education settings, integrated learning systems may be very effective (Falicki, 2000). Cary High School in Cary, North Carolina, uses an ILS in its Accelerated Learning Center. Students work at their own pace and on their own time. Students work 5 to 20 hours a week in addition to taking regular classes, to either advance more rapidly, or to stay on track with their peers.

Considering the huge expense to initiate and maintain ILS in schools, their use has frequently been limited to Chapter I students. Because of the "drill/practice" emphasis of the ILS software, critics wonder if low-income students are limited to less creative activities with the computer. On the other hand, in low-performing schools, ILS may enhance student performance sufficiently to warrant such investment.

One way of expanding access to ILS has been the use of cooperative learning in ILS environments. Most effective have been pairs of low achievers and high achievers, with enhanced learning outcomes for both members of the pair. Equally effective are pairs of high-achieving students. Less effective are homogeneous low-achieving pairs (Brush, 1997).

THE COMPUTER LAB

Most schools today have at least one room equipped with enough computers for a classroom-size group to work. However, many schools dilute whatever positive learning outcomes might result from computer activities in their efforts to provide egalitarian access to all students. Due to teacher reluctance to implement technology, many schools have opted to use a computer resource specialist who is responsible for computer learning. Unless the computer resource specialist works closely with classroom teachers, however, the meaningful integration of computer use with classroom curriculum is limited.

Schools that have been successful in increasing student learning outcomes with computer labs have:

1. provided adequate professional development so that teachers can design, plan, and implement the computer lessons. A computer resource teacher is invaluable to assist with technical support and trouble-shooting during lessons.

2. set up a schedule that accommodates different needs of students for various activities. Students need intensive, extended time at the computer for some activities (producing a draft of an essay or story) and continuity for others (20 minutes a day for four or five days a week for math drill and practice to develop fluency and speed on skills introduced and practiced under teacher guidance in the classroom).

3. considered the learning needs of the students in the computer lab environment. The computer lab is the ideal place for students to complete drafts of a composition, edit earlier work, and print final copies. Doing research on the Internet for a class project can be done effectively in a lab. However, most labs are not set up for small groups to share their work, or even for teachers to conduct discussions with the whole class about discoveries, challenges, or strategies that are working or not working. It is sometimes difficult to make sure that computers in the lab have exactly the right equipment a student might need. The teacher needs a station and projector to demonstrate and model, and he or she needs to be able to see at a glance what the students are doing, who's having trouble, and who's work needs to be shared with the class.

Teachers should not assume that the computer lab is the ideal place for a computer lesson. If you do need the lab to complete a lesson, think about ways your class can fit into the way the computer lab operates (or work to change the way the lab is set up or has been operated in the past).

THE ONE-COMPUTER CLASSROOM

For the teacher in a one-computer classroom, Dockterman (1997) suggests the following uses:

1. manage responsibilities and paperwork (IEPs, assessment reports, letters to parents);
2. make dazzling presentations (PowerPoint presentations, graphs of student data, time lines, mind-maps) using an LCD projector or a large-screen television;
3. lead incredible discussions; use simulation and role-playing software such as Decisions, Decisions to guide students in problem-solving activities in social studies;
4. manage dynamic cooperative learning activities: with students in cooperative groups and a program like Rainforest Researchers, students solve a problem watching segments of the situation on the large-screen monitor;
5. inspire enlightening self-discovery;
6. communicate with colleagues via E-mail.

Just as teachers will enjoy a sense of increased productivity in a classroom with a computer, students in the one-computer classroom can benefit by having an opportunity to do composing and editing as they need to, using a learning center for a small group project, seeking out an electronic tutor to practice intensively on a new skill, and doing research on the Internet for a class assignment.

THE CLASSROOM WITH SEVERAL COMPUTERS

Rather than (or in addition to) setting up a computer lab, some schools choose to place five or six computers in several classrooms of teachers who are particularly interested in integrating computer use on a regular basis. Using a computer projection device or large-screen television monitor, a teacher can instruct an entire class by using selected computer software to do a demonstration, list class ideas, and so on. Following the teacher presentation, students then work on application activities in small groups at the computers or rotate between computer and noncomputer activities. After the application activities, students meet again as a large group to compare responses, talk about progress and challenges, and deal with the interpersonal aspects of group work in addition to the content objectives of the lesson.

The strengths of the several-computers classroom is that it puts the computers where the students are, thereby allowing easy access to technology across subject areas. It also focuses the teacher as the designer of instruction, integrating computer use into curriculum objectives. The primary limitation of the model is the lack of adequate training for teachers in how to combine computer and noncomputer activities, selecting software that is best suited for this type of classroom and the targeted curriculum, and scheduling computer use for students that does not disrupt the lesson.

Without this training, many teachers have used the computer as a reward activity, with students using drill or game software after they have finished their "real" work, or have several students doing drill-and-practice work while the rest of the class works on something else. The software is usually chosen not for its educational value but because it is easy to use with little or no supervision by the teacher. This approach is called *computer accommodation,* in contrast to the recommended approach of *computer integration* (Gardner & Edyburn, 2000).

According to Pogrow (1988), there are three components of effective teaching with the computer:

1. teaching must be process-oriented, with students developing and testing their own ideas rather than being told what to do by the teacher;
2. teaching must force students to articulate their hypotheses and results, as well as cause-and-effect relationships. It is the articulation of conscious ideas that produces much of transferable learning, not just operating the software.
3. Teachers must integrate effective noncomputer teaching techniques with computer activities.

Figure 14.1 summarizes the types of technology facilities a school might choose to use and the benefits and limitations of each (Roblyer & Edwards, 2000).

DISTANCE LEARNING

Distance learning can be as sophisticated as taking an entire course on-line, or it can be as simple as connecting students in distant places who are working on the same project. National Geographic's Kids Network uses E-mail to link students doing collaborative investigations and data collection and analysis. Stanford University offers advanced math, physics, and writing courses to students in middle and high schools (Dale, 2000).

These experiences may be conducted in "real-time" so that students can ask the teachers questions and get immediate feedback, or they can be provided "asynchronously," or at times convenient for the students. E-mail and electronic bulletin boards allow students to communicate privately with each other and the instructor, or publicly by posting responses on a bulletin board.

PORTABLE LABS (LAPTOPS, NOTEBOOKS, AND PERSONAL DIGITAL ASSISTANTS)

Notebook and laptop computers and personal digital assistants, such as the Palm Pilot™ are changing the tools students use for their daily work. "Studies are showing that these high-tech tools are making a profoundly positive impact on teaching and learning" (Healey, 1999, p. 14). According to a series of studies done with more than 450 students, in classrooms where notebook computers are used, students demonstrate more problem-solving and critical-thinking skills and use a greater number of information sources in research projects.

FIGURE 14.1 Types of Technology Facilities and their Uses

	BENEFITS/POSSIBILITIES	LIMITATIONS/PROBLEMS	COMMON USES
Labs	Centralized resources are easier to maintain and keep secure; software can be networked and shared	Need permanent staff to supervise and maintain resources; students must leave classrooms	See below
Special Purpose Labs	Permanent setups; group resources specific to the needs of certain content areas or types of students	Usually exclude other groups; isolate resources	Programming courses, word-processing classes, keyboarding, science labs, vocational courses, low achieving students, multimedia production courses
General-use labs	Accommodate varied uses by different groups	Difficult to schedule specific uses; usually available to only one class at a time	Student productivity tasks (reports, assignments), class demonstrations, follow-up work
Library-media center labs	Same as general-use labs, but permanent staff are already present; ready access to all materials to promote integration of computer and noncomputer resources	Same as general use labs; staff will need special training; classes cannot do production or other group work that may bother other users of the library/media center	Same as general use labs
Mobile workstations	Stretch resources by sharing them among many users	Moving equipment increases breakage and other maintenance problem; difficult to get through doors or up stairs; security problems	Demonstrations
Mobile PCs (laptops)	On-demand access	Portability increases security problems	Individual student or teacher production tasks; teachers' assessment tasks
Classroom workstations	Easily accessible to teachers and students	No immediate assistance available to teachers; only a few students can use at one time	Tutoring and drills; demonstrations; production tasks for cooperative learning groups; E-mail with other teachers
Stand-alone classroom computers	Easily accessible to teachers and students	Same as classroom workstations	Tutoring and drills; whole-class demonstrations; pairs/ small work groups

From *Integrating Educational Technology into Teaching* by M.Roblyer & J. Edwards, 2000, p. 38. Reprinted with permission of Prentice-Hall.

Teachers report that writing skills have improved, and the overall quality of academic work has increased (Healey, 1999). An additional benefit of portable computers is that students who need particular adaptive devices can have their computers with them wherever they go, so that they can participate in computing alongside their peers (Garber & Rein, 2000).

AFTER-SCHOOL LEARNING/COMPUTER CLUBS

With a substantial investment in hardware and software, many schools are eager to get the most from their money by opening up opportunities to access technology to students, their families, and the community after school hours. For some students, these opportunities can mean the difference between supervised and wholesome activities and the kinds of trouble students can get into, unsupervised, after school.

Project KLICK is a federally funded project that has established after-school community learning centers in Michigan. Typical activities in such a computer clubhouse include building personal Web pages, making Web sites for businesses, filming and editing digital movies, creating PowerPoint presentations, and burning their finished products into a CD-ROM. Some of the outcomes from these centers include improved academic achievement, communication, collaboration, creative and critical thinking, strengthened relationships between school and community, and increased understanding and sharing across generations (Girod & Zhao, 2000).

A creative outcome of one KLICK community was the Adopt-a-Teacher program, in which teachers needing computer advice or assistance could be adopted by a clubhouse member volunteering her or his time and energy after school. One student "adopted" her seventh-grade social studies teacher by finding amazing stories about what happened to the men who signed the Declaration of Independence. Helen used her desktop publishing skills to make class handouts that were clearer and more interesting than their textbook. "The other students were really impressed with Helen's skills and enjoyed the handouts so much more than the book. We all came out ahead." KLICK not only provided an opportunity for Helen to learn technology skills and share them with her teacher, but she also benefited by gaining the respect of her classmates.

THE SCHOOLWIDE TECHNOLOGY PLAN

At the heart of every successful school's implementation of technology is the *technology plan*. Based on the work you did in the last chapter—formulating a vision that will guide your work—your school (as well as your district) must establish an on-going technology planning process.

Who should be a part of the technology planning process? Educators, technology experts, parents, and representatives of school district administration (so that school and district planning will be compatible, and the school can take advantage of expertise and cost effectiveness factors for purchasing). The core committee might be small, with frequent input and feedback from a larger advisory group. A heterogeneous group that includes both technophobes and technophiles will ensure that a range of opinions is heard (Hasselbring & Bottge, 2000). Technology must be viewed as a "core value" if it is to work effectively in the school system or individual school (Kwajewski, 1997).

The next step should be to write a student-centered mission statement that uses the vision as its touchstone (Reksten, 2000). Beginning with the outcomes for students avoids the pitfalls of starting with equipment, which allows participants to lose sight of the vision. The mission statement from Walt Disney School in Anaheim, California, for example, states:

> All students will become competent in using technology as a tool to enhance curriculum projects that support the integration of process skills in oral and written communication, calculations, solving problems, research, organization, and presentation of information. All students will learn to access and use Internet resources for technology-enhanced curriculum projects cooperatively, ethically, and collaboratively. All students will have opportunities to produce and share technology-enhanced curriculum projects cooperatively, ethically, and collaboratively (Reksten, 2000, p. 46).

Reksten suggests establishing benchmarks and expectations for students so that it is clear what technology resources will be required to implement the plan. The next step should be an assessment of current status and anticipated needs (analysis of the discrepancy of "what is" and "what should be").

Teacher training, technical support, and addressing equity issues are also important components of the technology plan (Roblyer & Edwards, 2000). Building in an evaluation system so that the plan can be reviewed in light of student and teacher outcomes will be an invaluable tool in applying for external funding and for reporting results to all the stakeholders.

Careful planning, involvement of stakeholders in deciding the type and amount of resources available for technology, flexibility in implementation, and ongoing evaluation and action research to examine what works and what doesn't are keys to successful implementation and integration in the inclusive school.

STUDENT ACTIVITIES

1. Obtain a copy of your school or district technology plan. Does it have a vision? How does the vision compare with the activity you completed in Chapter 13?

2. Make a list of the different types of access to technology available in your school (computer lab, one-computer classrooms, multicomputer classrooms, etc.). Given the number of students in your school, calculate the number of minutes per week each student theoretically has access to computers. What is the reality of the access per student?

3. List the provisions of the plan for technology access for students with special needs.

4. Brainstorm a list of ideas you would want to propose, based on reading this book and your own experience, for the revision of your school or district technology plan.

REFERENCES

Becker, H., & Sterling, C. (1987). Equity in school computer use: National data and neglected considerations. *Journal of Educational Computing Research, 3,* 289–311.
Brush, T. (1997). The effects of group composition on achievement and time on task for students completing ILS activities in cooperative pairs. *Journal of Research on Computing in Education, 30,* 2–17.

Dale, E. (2000). Technology for individuals with gifts and talents. In J. Lindsey (Ed.), *Technology & exceptional individuals*. Austin, TX: Pro-Ed.

Dockterman, D. (1997). *Great teaching in the one-computer classroom*. Watertown, MA: Tom Snyder Productions.

Falicki, S. (2000). Comprehensive courseware: A shining light for special student populations. *Media & Methods, 36*(4), 8–9.

Garber, S., & Rein, J. (2000). Access to technology: Removing hardware and other barriers. In J. Lindsey (Ed.), *Technology & exceptional individuals*. Austin, TX: Pro-Ed.

Gardner, J., & Edyburn, D. (2000). Integrating technology to support effective instruction. In J. Lindsey (Ed.), *Technology & exceptional individuals*. (pp. 000). Austin, TX: Pro-Ed.

Girod, M., & Zhao, Y. (2000). The Kulture of KLICK! *T.H.E. Journal. 27*(7), 70–72, 74, 76.

Hasselbring, T., & Bottge, B. (2000). Planning and implementing technology programs in inclusive settings. In J. Lindsey (Ed.), *Technology & exceptional individuals*. (pp. 000). Austin, TX: Pro-Ed, 91–113.

Healey, T. (1999). Notebook programs pave the way to student-centered learning. *T.H.E. Journal, 26*(9), 14.

Kwajewski, K. (1997). Technology as a core value. *Learning and Leading with Technology, 24*(5), 54–56.

Mevarech, Z. (1994). The effectiveness of individualized versus cooperative computer-based integrated learning systems. *International Journal of Educational Research, 21*(1), 12–15.

Pogrow, S. (1988). How to use computers to truly enhance learning. *Electronic Learning. 7*(8), 6–7.

Reksten, L. (2000). Using technology to increase student learning. Thousand Oaks, CA: Corwin Press.

Roblyer, M., & Edwards, J. (2000). *Integrating educational technology into teaching*. Upper Saddle River, NJ: Prentice-Hall.

Wiberg, K. (1995). Integrated learning systems: What does the research say? *The Computing Teacher, 22*(5), 7–10.

STATE ASSISTIVE TECHNOLOGY
PROJECT CONTACTS

ORGANIZATION	CONTACT INFORMATION
Alabama Statewide Technology Access and Response Project (STAR) System for Alabamians with Disabilities	2125 East South Boulevard P.O. Box 20752 Montgomery, AL 36120-0752 Project Director: Dr. Tom Gannaway Telephone: (334) 613-3480 or (800) STAR656 (In-State only); Fax: (334) 613-3485 Internet: *http://www.mindspring.com/~alstar* E-mail: alstar@mont.mindspring.com
American Samoa Assistive Technology Project	Division of Vocational Rehabilitation Department of Human Resources Pago Pago, American Samoa 96799 Project Director: Edmund Pereira Telephone: Voice (684) 699-1529; TDD (684) 233-7874; Fax: (684) 699-1376
Arizona Technology Access Program (AZTAP)	Institute for Human Development Northern Arizona University P.O. Box 5630 Flagstaff, AZ 86011 Information and Referral: ElizBeth Pifer Interim Director: Daniel Davidson, Ph.D. Telephone: Voice (520) 523-7035; TDD: (520) 523-1695; Fax: (520) 523-9127 Internet: *http://www.nau.edu/~ihd/aztap.html* E-mail: daniel.davidson@nau.edu
Arkansas Increasing Capabilities Access Network	Department of Education Vocational and Technical Education Division Arkansas Rehabilitation Services 2201 Brookwood Drive, Suite 117 Little Rock, AR 72202 Project Director: Sue Gaskin Telephone: Voice/TDD (501) 666-8868; Voice/TDD (800) 828-2799 (in-state only); Fax: (501) 666-5319 Internet: *http://www.arkansas-ican.org* E-mail: 102503.3602@compuserve.com

ORGANIZATION	CONTACT INFORMATION
Assistive Technologies of Alaska	701 E. Tudor Road, Suite 280 Anchorage, AK 99503-7445 Information and Referral: Rose Foster Telephone: Voice/TDD (907) 563-0138 Program Director: Michael Shiffer Telephone: Voice/TDD (907) 274-5606; Fax: (907) 274-5605 Internet: *http//:www.corcom.com/ata/index.html*
California Assistive Technology System	California Department of Rehabilitation (Lead Agency) 830 K Street, Room 102 Sacramento, CA 95814 Mailing Address: P.O. Box 944222 Sacramento, CA 94244-2220 Information and Referral: Kent Gregory Telephone: Voice (800) 390-2699 Project Director: Catherine Campisi Project Coordinator: Dennis Law Telephone: Voice/TDD (916) 324-3062; Fax: (916) 323-0914 Internet: *http://www.catsca.com* E-mail: doroa.ccampisi@hw1.cahwnet.gov
Colorado Assistive Technology Project	Rocky Mountain Resource and Training Institute 1391 N. Speer Boulevard, Suite 350 Denver, CO 80204 Information Operator: Judith Volkman Project Director: Cathy Bodine Telephone: Voice (303) 534-1027; TDD (303) 534-1063; Fax: (303) 534-1075 E-mail: cathy.bodine@uchsc.edu
Connecticut Assistive Technology Project	Bureau of Rehabilitation Services 10 Griffin Road North Windsor, CT 06095 Project Director: John M. Ficarro Telephone: Voice (860) 298-2014; TDD (860) 298-2018; Fax: (860) 298-9590 Internet: *http://www.ucc.uconn.edu/~techact/* E-mail: cttap@aol.com
Delaware Assistive Technology Initiative (DATI)	Applied Science & Engineering Laboratories University of Delaware Dupont Hospital for Children 1600 Rockland Road, Room 154 P.O. BOX 269 Wilmington, DE 19899-0269 Project Director: Beth A. Mineo Mollica, Ph.D. Telephone: Voice (302) 651-6790; TDD (302) 651-6794; Fax: (302) 651-6793

ORGANIZATION	CONTACT INFORMATION
Delaware Assistive Technology Initiative (DATI) *(continued)*	Internet: *http://www.asel.udel.edu/dati* E-mail: dati@asel.udel.edu
D.C. Partnership for Assistive Technology	801 Pennsylvania Avenue, SE, Suite 300 Washington, D.C. 20003 Information Specialist: Alex Lugo Project Director: Jody Wildy Telephone: Voice (202) 546-9163; TDD (202) 546-9168; Fax: (202) 546-9169
Florida Alliance for Assistive Service and Technology	2002-A Old Saint Augustine Road Tallahassee, FL 32399-0696 Project Director: Terry Ward Telephone: Voice/TDD (904) 487-3278; Fax: (904) 921-7214 E-mail: faast@freenet.scri.fsu.edu
Georgia Tools for Life	Division of Rehabilitation Services 2 Peachtree Street, N.W., Suite 35-413 Atlanta, GA 30303-3166 Project Director: Joy Kniskern Telephone: Voice (404) 657-3084, (800) 578-8665 (in-state only); TDD (404) 657-3085 Fax: (404) 657-3086 E-mail: 102476.1737@compuserve.com
Guam System for Assistive Technology	University Affiliated Program—Developmental Disabilities House #12 Dean's Circle University of Guam UOG Station Mangilao, Guam 96923 Principal Investigator: Heidi E. Farra-San Nicolas, Ph.D. Project Director: Ben Servino Telephone: Voice (671) 735-2493; TDD (671) 734-8378; Fax: (671) 734-5709 E-mail: uapservi@uog.edu
Hawaii Assistive Technology Training and Services (HATTS)	414 Kuwili Street, Suite 104 Honolulu, HI 96817 Information and Referral: Judith Clark Telephone: Voice (808) 532-7114 Project Director: Barbara Fischlowitz-Leong, M.Ed. Telephone: Voice/TDD (808) 532-7110; Fax: (808) 532-7120 E-mail: bfl@pixi.com
Idaho Assistive Technology Project	129 W. Third Street Moscow, ID 83843 Information and Referral: Michelle Doty Telephone: Voice (208) 885-3630 Project Director: Ron Seiler Telephone: Voice/TDD (208) 885-3559; Fax: (208) 885-3628 E-mail: seile861@uidaho.edu

ORGANIZATION	CONTACT INFORMATION
Illinois Assistive Technology Project	528 S. 5th Street, Suite 100 Springfield, IL 62701 Project Director: Wilhelmina Gunther Telephone: Voice (217) 522-7985; TDD (217) 522-9966; Fax: (217) 522-8067 E-mail: gunther@midwest.net

Indiana ATTAIN (Accessing Technology through Awareness in Indiana) Project	1815 N. Meridian, Suite 200
	Indianapolis, IN 46202
	Project Manager: Cris Fulford
	Telephone: Voice (317) 921-8766 (Marion County),
	   (800) 528-8246 (in-state only); TDD (800) 743-3333 (National);
	   Fax: (317) 921-8774
	E-mail: cfulford@vunet.vinu.edu

Iowa Program for Assistive Technology	Iowa University Affiliated Program University Hospital School Iowa City, IA 52242-1011 Information and Referral: Amy Hanna Telephone: Voice (319) 356-1514 Co-Director: Mary Quigley Telephone: Voice (319) 356-4402 Telephone: Voice/TDD (800) 331-3027 (National); Fax: (319) 356-8284 E-mail: mary_quigley@uiowa.edu
Assistive Technology for Kansans Project	2601 Gabriel P.O. Box 738 Parsons, KS 67357 Project Director: Charles R. Spellman Project Coordinator: Sheila Simmons Telephone: Voice (316) 421-8367 or (800) KAN DO IT; Fax/TDD: (316) 421-0954
Kentucky Assistive Technology Services Network	Charles McDowell Rehabilitation Center 8412 Westport Road Louisville, KY 40242 Information and Referral: Jerry Wheatley Project Director: J. Chase Forrester Telephone: Voice (502) 327-0022; TDD (502) 327-9855 or Voice/TDD (800) 327-5287 (in-state only); Fax: (502) 327-9974 Internet: *http://www.katsnet.org* E-mail: katsnet@iglou.com
Louisiana Assistive Technology Access Network	P.O. Box 14115 Baton Rouge, LA 70898-4115 Executive Director: Julie Nesbit Telephone: Voice/TDD (504) 925-9500 or Voice/TDD (800) 270-6185; Fax: (504) 925-9560 E-mail: latanstate@aol.com

ORGANIZATION	CONTACT INFORMATION
Maine Consumer Information and Technology Training Exchange (Maine CITE)	Maine CITE Coordinating Center Education Network of Maine 46 University Drive Augusta, ME 04330 Project Director: Kathy Powers Telephone: Voice/TDD (207) 621-3195; Fax: (207) 621-3193 E-mail: kpowers@maine.caps.maine.edu
Maryland Technology Assistance Program	Governor's Office for Individuals with Disabilities 300 W. Lexington Street, Box 10 Baltimore, MD 21201 Information and Referral: James Corey Telephone: Voice (800) TECH-TAP Project Director: Mary Brady, M.S. Telephone: Voice/TDD (410) 333-4975; Fax: (410) 333-6674 Internet: *http://www/clark.net/pub/mdtap* E-mail: mdtap@clark.net
Massachusetts Assistive Technology Partnership	MATP Center Children's Hospital 1295 Boylston Streét, Suite 310 Boston, MA 02115 Information and Referral: Patricia Hill Telephone: Voice (617) 355-7153 or Voice/TDD (800) 848-8867 (in-state only) Project Director: Judy Brewer Telephone: Voice (617) 355-6380; TDD (617) 355-7301; Fax: (617) 355-6345 E-mail: brewer_ju@a1.tch.harvard.edu
Michigan Tech 2000	Michigan Assistive Technology Project 3815 West Saint Joseph Highway Lansing, MI 48917-3623 Project Director: Sheryl Avery-Meints Project Manager: Mary Barnes Telephone: Voice (517) 334-6502; TDD (517) 334-6499; Fax: (517) 373-0565
Minnesota STAR Program	300 Centennial Building 658 Cedar Street St. Paul, MN 55155 Executive Director: Rachel Wobschall Telephone: Voice (612) 296-2771 or (800) 657-3862 (in-state only); TDD (612) 296-8478; Fax: (612) 282-6671 Internet: *http://www.state.mn.us/ebranch/admin/ assistivetechnology.html* E-mail: mnstars@edu.gte.net

ORGANIZATION	CONTACT INFORMATION
Mississippi Project START	P.O. Box 1000 Jackson, MS 39205-1000 Information and Referral: Albert Newsome Telephone: Voice (601) 987-4872 Project Director: Stephen Power Telephone: Voice (601) 853-5171;Voice/TDD (800) 852-8328 (in-state only); Fax: (601) 364-2349 E-mail: spower@netdoor.com
Missouri Assistive Technology Project	4731 South Cochise, Suite 114 Independence, MO 64055-6975 Project Director: Diane Golden, Ph.D. Telephone: Voice (816) 373-5193 or (800) 647-8557 (in-state only); TDD (816) 373-9315; Fax: (816) 373-9314 E-mail: matpmo@qni.com
MONTECH	MUARID, The University of Montana 634 Eddy Avenue Missoula, MT 59812 Project Director: Peter Leech Telephone: Voice (800) 732-0323 (National); TDD (406) 243-5676; Fax: (406) 243-4730 E-mail: montech@selway.umt.edu
Nebraska Assistive Technology Project	301 Centennial Mall South P.O. Box 94987 Lincoln, NE 68509-4987 Information and Referral: Kathryn Kruse Telephone: Voice/TDD (402) 471-2447 Project Director: Mark Schultz Telephone: Voice/TDD (402) 471-0735 Telephone: Voice (800) 742-7594 (in-state only); Fax: (402) 471-0117 Internet: *http://www.nde.state.ne.us/atp/techome.html* E-mail: mschultz@nde4.nde.state.ne.us
Nevada Assistive Technology Collaborative	Rehabilitation Division Office of Community Based Services 711 South Stewart Street Carson City, NV 89710 Information and Referral: Todd Butterworth Project Administrator: Donny Loux Telephone: Voice (702) 687-4452; TDD (702) 687-3388; Fax: (702) 687-3292 Internet: *http://www.state.nv.us.80* E-mail: nvreach@powernet.net

ORGANIZATION	CONTACT INFORMATION
New Hampshire Technology Partnership Project	Institute on Disability/UAP #14 Ten Ferry Street The Concord Center Concord, NH 03301 Information and Referral: Carol Richards Telephone: Voice/TDD (603) 224-0630 Project Director: Jan Nisbet Telephone: Voice (603) 862-4320 Project Coordinator: Marion Pawlek Telephone: Voice/TDD (603) 224-0630; Fax: (603) 226-0389 E-mail: mjpawlek@christa.unh.edu
New Jersey Technology Assistive Resource Program (TARP)	135 East State Street CN 398 Trenton, NJ 08625 Project Director: Interim Project Director Telephone: Voice (800) 922-7233; (609) 292-7498; TDD (800) 382-7765; Fax: (609) 292-8347 E-mail: PaulJZ@aol.com
New Mexico Technology Assistance Program	435 St. Michael's Drive, Building D Santa Fe, NM 87503 Information and Referral: Carol Cadena Telephone: Voice/TDD (800) 866-ABLE Project Director: Alan Klaus Telephone: Voice/TDD (505) 827-3532; Fax: (505) 827-3746 E-mail: nmdvrtap@aol.com
New York State TRAID Project	Office of Advocate for Persons with Disabilities One Empire State Plaza, Suite 1001 Albany, NY 12223-1150 Project Director: Deborah Buck Telephone: Voice (518) 474-2825; Voice/TDD (800) 522-4369 (in-state only) TDD (518) 473-4231; Fax: (518) 473-6005 E-mail: d.buck@oapwd.state.ny.us
North Carolina Assistive Technology Project	Department of Human Resources Division of Vocational Rehabilitation Services 1110 Navaho Drive, Suite 101 Raleigh, NC 27609-7322 Information and Referral Telephone: Voice (800) 852-0042 (National) Project Director: Ricki Cook Telephone: Voice/TDD (919) 850-2787; Fax: (919) 850-2792 Internet: *http://www.mindspring.com/~ncatp* E-mail: rickic@mindspring.com

ORGANIZATION	CONTACT INFORMATION
North Dakota Interagency Program for Assistive Technology (IPAT)	P.O. Box 743 Cavalier, ND 58220 Director: Judie Lee Telephone: Voice/TDD (701) 265-4807; Fax: (701) 265-3150 E-mail: lee@pioneer.state.nd.us
Commonwealth of the Northern Mariana Islands Assistive Technology Project	Developmental Disabilities Planning Office Office of the Governor, Building 1312 P.O. Box 2565 Saipan, MP 96950 Project Director: Thomas J. Camacho Telephone: Voice/TDD (670) 322-3014; Fax: (670) 322-4168 E-mail: dd.council@saipan.com
Ohio TRAIN	Ohio Super Computer Center 1224 Kinnear Road Columbus, OH 43212 Information Specialist: Marie Kahl Telephone: Voice (614) 292-2426 Executive Director: Douglas Huntt Telephone: Voice (614) 292-2426; Voice/TDD (800) 784-3425 (in-state only); TDD (614) 292-3162; Fax: (614) 292-5866 Internet: *http://train.ovl.osc.edu* E-mail: huntt.1@osu.edu
Oklahoma ABLE Tech	Oklahoma State University Wellness Center 1514 W. Hall of Fame Road Stillwater, OK 74078-2026 Project Manager: Linda Jaco Telephone: Voice (405) 744-9864 or (405) 744-9748 or Voice/TDD (800) 257-1705; Fax: (405) 744-7670 Internet: *http://www.okstate.edu/wellness/at-home.htm* E-mail: mljwell@okway.okstate.edu
Oregon Technology Access for Life Needs Project (TALN)	1257 Ferry Street, SE Salem, OR 97310 Project Director: Byron McNaught Telephone: Voice/TDD (503) 361-1201; Fax: (503) 378-3599 E-mail: ati@orednet.org
Pennsylvania's Initiative on Assistive Technology	Institute on Disabilities/UAP Ritter Annex 433 Philadelphia, PA 19122 Information and Referral: Lynn Zelvin Telephone: Voice (215) 204-5966 Project Director: Amy Goldman Telephone: Voice/TDD (215) 204-5968 or (800) 750-PIAT (TT); Fax: (215) 204-9371 E-mail: piat@astro.ocis.temple.edu

ORGANIZATION	CONTACT INFORMATION
Puerto Rico Assistive Technology Project	University of Puerto Rico Medical Sciences Campus College of Related Health Professions Office of Project Investigation and Development Box 365067 San Juan, PR 00936-5067 Project Director: Maria I. Miranda, B.A. Telephone: Voice (809) 758-2525, ext. 4413 or (800) 496-6035 (from U.S. only) or (800) 981-6033 (in PR only); TDD/Fax: (809) 754-8034
Rhode Island Assistive Technology Access Project	Office of Rehabilitation Services 40 Fountain Street Providence, RI 02903-1898 Project Director: Susan Olson Telephone: Voice (401) 421-7005 or (800) 752-8088, ext. 2608 (in-state only); TDD (401) 421-7016; Fax: (401) 274-1920 Internet: *http://www.ors.state.ri.us.* E-mail: ab195@osfn.rhilinet.gov
South Carolina Assistive Technology Program	USC School of Medicine Center for Developmental Disabilities Columbia, SC 29208 Project Director: Evelyn Evans Telephone: Voice (803) 935-5240 Telephone: Voice/TDD (803) 935-5263; Fax: (803) 935-5342 Internet: *http://www.cdd.sc.edu/scatp/scatp.htm* E-mail: scatp@scsn.net
South Dakota Assistive Technology Project (DAKOTALINK)	1925 Plaza Boulevard Rapid City, SD 57702 Project Director: Ron Reed, Ph.D. Telephone: Voice (605) 394-1876 or (800) 645-0673 (in-state only); Fax: (605) 394-5315 Internet: *http://www.tie.net/dakotalink* E-mail: rreed@sdtie.sdserv.org
Tennessee Technology Access Project	710 James Robertson Parkway Andrew Johnson Tower, 10th Floor Nashville, TN 37243-0675 Information and Referral: Anastasia Koshakji Project Director: Rob Roberts, Ph.D. Telephone: Voice (615) 532-6558 or (800) 732-5059 (in-state only); TDD (615) 741-4566; Fax: (615) 532-6719 E-mail: rroberts2@mail.state.tn.us

ORGANIZATION	CONTACT INFORMATION
Texas Assistive Technology Partnership	University of Texas at Austin College of Education SZ8252-D5100 Austin, TX 78712-1290 Information and Referral: John Moore Telephone: Voice (800) 828-7839 Interim Project Director: Susanne Elrod Telephone Voice (512) 471-7621; TDD (512) 471-1844; Fax: (512) 471-7549 Internet: *http://www.edb.utexas.edu/coe/depts/sped/tatp/tatp.html* E-mail: s.elrod@mail.utexas.edu
U.S. Virgin Island Technology-Related Assistance for Individuals with Disabilities (TRAID)	University of the Virgin Islands/UAP #2 John Brewers Bay St. Thomas, VI 00801-0990 Executive Director: Dr. Yegin Habteyes Telephone: Voice (809) 693-1323; Fax: (809) 693-1325 E-mail: yhabtey@gecko.uvi.edu
Utah Assistive Technology Program	Center for Persons with Disabilities UMC 6855 Logan, UT 84322-6855 Project Director: Marvin Fifield, Ed.D. Telephone: Voice (801) 797-1982 or (801) 797-3824; TDD (801) 797-2096; Fax: (801) 797-2355 E-mail: Pending Update
Vermont Assistive Technology Project	103 South Main Street Weeks Building, First Floor Waterbury, VT 05671-2305 Project Director: Lynne Cleveland Telephone: Voice/TDD (802) 241-2620; Fax: (802) 241-3052 Internet: *http://www.uvm.edu/~uapvt/cats.html* E-mail: lynnec@dad.state.vt.us
Virginia Assistive Technology System	8004 Franklin Farms Drive P.O. Box K300 Richmond, VA 23288-0300 Information and Referral: Maureen Kelly-Olson Telephone: Voice (757) 552-5019 Project Director: Kenneth Knorr Telephone: Voice/TDD (757) 662-9990; Fax: (804) 662-9478 E-mail: vatskhk@aol.com

ORGANIZATION	CONTACT INFORMATION
Washington Assistive Technology Alliance	DSHS/DVR P.O. Box 45340 Olympia, WA 98504-5340 Project Director: Debbie Cook Telephone: Voice (206) 685-4181 Telephone: Voice (360) 438-8000; TDD (360) 438-8644; Fax: (360) 438-8007 Internet: *http:/weber.u.washington.edu/~atrc* E- mail: debcook@u.washington.edu
West Virginia Assistive Technology System	University Affiliated Center for Developmental Disabilities Airport Research and Office Park 955 Hartman Run Road Morgantown, WV 26505 Project Manager: Jack Stewart Telephone: Voice/TDD (304) 293-4692 or Voice (800) 841-8436 (in-state only); Fax: (304) 293-7294 E-mail: stewiat@wvnvm.wvnet.edu
WISTECH	Division of Supportive Living 2917 International Lane, 3rd Floor Madison, WI 53704 Project Director: Susan Kidder Telephone: Voice (608) 243-5675 Telephone: Voice/TDD (608) 243-5674; Fax: (608) 243-5681
Wyoming's New Options in Technology (WYNOT)	P.O. Box 4298 Laramie, WY 82071-4298 Co-Project Director: Kirk McKinney Telephone: Voice (307) 777-6947 Co-Project Director: Thomas McVeigh Telephone: Voice (307) 766-2764 Telephone: Voice/TDD (307) 777-4386 or 777-7450; Fax: (307) 777-5939 Internet: *http://www.uwyo.edu/hs/wind/wynot/wynot.htm* E-mail: kmckin@missc.state.wy.us

ATA RESOURCE CENTERS

ALABAMA

Birmingham Alliance for Technology Access Center
Birmingham Independent Living Center
206 13th Street South
Birmingham, AL 35233-1317
(205) 251-2223 (Voice/TTY)
E-mail: mikenorris@mindspring.net
Mike Norris

Technology Assistance for Special Consumers
P.O. Box 443
Huntsville, AL 35804
(256) 532-5996 (Voice/TTY)
E-mail: tasc@traveller.com
WWW: *http://tasc.ataccess.org*
Glenda Anderson

ARIZONA

Technology Access Center of Tucson
4710 East 29th Street
P.O. Box 13178
Tucson, AZ 85732-3178
(520) 745-5588, ext.412
E-mail: tactaz@aol.com
Paula Feeney

ARKANSAS

Technology Resource Center
c/o Arkansas Easter Seal Society
3920 Woodland Heights Road
Little Rock, AR 72212-2495

(501)227-3602
E-mail: atrce@aol.com
Joe Glover

CALIFORNIA

Center for Accessible Technology
2547 8th St., 12-A
Berkeley, CA 94710-2572
(510) 841-3224 (Voice/TTY)
E-mail: info@cforat.org
WWW: *http://www.el.net/CAT*
Dmitri Belser

Computer Access Center
6234 West 87th Street
Los Angeles, CA 90045
(310) 338-1597
E-mail: cac@cac.org
WWW: *http://www.cac.org*
Mary Ann Glicksman

iTECH—Parents Helping Parents
3041 Olcott Street
Santa Clara, CA 95054-3222
(408) 727-5775
E-mail: iTech@php.com
WWW: *http://www.php.com*
Angela Patterson

San Diego Assistive Technology Center
UCP of San Diego County
3821 Calle Fortunada, Suite C
San Diego, CA 92123
(858) 571-7803
E-mail: ucpsdatc@pacbell.net
Kristin White

Team of Advocates for Special Kids
100 W. Cerritos Ave.
Anaheim, CA 92805
(714) 533-8275
E-mail: taskca@yahoo.com
Laura Grieef

FLORIDA

CITE, Inc.—Center for Independence,Technology, & Education
215 E. New Hampshire St.
Orlando, FL 32804
(407) 898-2483
E-mail: citeinfo@cite-fl.com
Lee Nasehi

GEORGIA

Tech-Able, Inc.
1114 Brett Drive, Suite 100
Conyers, GA 30094
(770) 922-6768
E-mail: techable@america.net
Carolyn McGonagill

HAWAII

Aloha Special Technology Access Center
710 Green St.
Honolulu, HI 96813
(808) 523-5547
E-mail: astachi@yahoo.com
WWW: *http://www.geocities.com/astachi/index.html*
Eric Arveson

IDAHO

United Cerebral Palsy of Idaho, Inc.
5530 West Emerald
Boise, ID 83706
(208) 377-8070
E-mail: ucpidaho@aol.com
WWW: *http://ucpidaho.ataccess.org*
Pat Harting

ILLINOIS

Northern Illinois Center for Adaptive Technology
3615 Louisiana Road
Rockford, IL 61108-6195

(815) 229-2163
E-mail: davegrass@earthlink.net
WWW: *nicat.ataccess.org*
Dave Grass

Technical Aids & Assistance for the Disabled Center
1950 West Roosevelt Road
Chicago, IL 60608
(312) 421-3373 (Voice/TTY)
E-mail: taad@interaccess.com
WWW: *http://homepage.interaccess.com/~taad*
Diedre Pate

INDIANA

Assistive Technology Training and Information Center
Attic: A Resource Center on Independent Living
3354 Pine Hill Dr.
P.O. Box 2441
Vincennes, IN 47591
(812) 886-0575 (Voice/TTY)
E-mail: inattic1@aol.com
WWW: *www.theattic.org*
Pat Stewart

KANSAS

Technology Resource Solutions for People
1710 West Schilling Road
Salina, KS 67402-1160
(785) 827-9383
E-mail: trspks@midusa.net
Kathy Reed

KENTUCKY

Bluegrass Technology Center
961 Beasley Street, Ste. 103A
Lexington, KY 40509-4120
(859) 294-4343
(800) 209-7767 (KY)

E-mail: office@bluegrass-tech.org
WWW: *http://www.bluegrass-tech.org*
Bob Glass

EnTech: Enabling Technologies of Kentuckiana
Louisville Free Public Library
301 York Street
Louisville, KY 40203-2257
(502) 574-1637
(800) 890-1840 (KY)
E-mail: entech@iglou.com
WWW: *http://www.kde.state.ky.us/oet/customer/at/*
Sandi Baker

Western Kentucky Assistive Technology Consortium
P.O. Box 266
Murray, KY 42071
(270) 759-4233
E-mail: wkatc@cablecomm-ky.net
WWW: *http://www.kde.state.ky.us/oet/customer/at/*
Melissa Miller

MARYLAND

Learning Independence through Computers, Inc. (LINC)
1001 Eastern Avenue, 3rd floor
Baltimore, MD 21202
(410) 659-5462 (Voice)
(410) 659-5472 (Fax/TTY)
E-mail: info@linc.org
WWW: *http://www.linc.org*
Mary Salkever

MICHIGAN

Michigan's Assistive Technology Resource
1023 S. US 27, Suite B31
St. Johns, MI 48879
(517) 224-0333 Voice or TDD
(800) 274-7426 (MI) Voice or TDD
E-mail: matr@match.org
WWW: *www.matr.org*
Maryann Jones

MINNESOTA

PACER Computer Resource Center
4826 Chicago Avenue South
Minneapolis, MN 55417-1098
(612) 827-2966 (Voice/TTY)
E-mail: jpeters@pacer.org
WWW: *http://www.pacer.org/crc/crc.htm*
Janet Peters

MONTANA

Parents, Let's Unite for Kids (PLUK)
516 N 32nd St
Billings MT 59101
(406) 255-0540
(800) 222-7585 (MT)
E-mail: plukinfo@pluk.org
WWW: *http://www.pluk.org*
Roger Holt

NEW JERSEY

TECH Connection
Assistive Technology Solutions
c/o Family Resource Associates, Inc.
35 Haddon Avenue
Shrewsbury, NJ 07702-4007
(732) 747-5310
E-mail: tecconn@aol.com
WWW: *http://www.techconnection.org/*
Joanne Castellano

Center for Enabling Technology
622 Route 10 West, Suite 22B
Whippany, NJ 07981-0272
(973) 428-1455 (Voice)
(973) 428-1450 (TTY)
E-mail: cetnj@aol.com
WWW: *cetnj.ataccess.org*
Theresa Lupo

NEW YORK

Techspress Resource Center for Independent Living
P.O. Box 210
401–409 Columbia Street
Utica, NY 13503-0210
(315) 797-4642
E-mail: rose.roberts@rcil.com
Rose Roberts

NORTH CAROLINA

Carolina Computer Access Center
Metro School
700 East Second Street
Charlotte, NC 28202-2826
(704) 342-3004
E-mail: ccacnc@aol.com
WWW: *http://ccac.ataccess.org*
Judy Timms

OHIO

Technology Resource Center
Job Mall
1133 Edwin C. Moses Blvd., Suite 370
Dayton, OH 45408
(937) 461-3305
E-mail: trcdoh@aol.com
Pat Cashdollar

RHODE ISLAND

TechACCESS Center of Rhode Island
110 Jefferson Blvd.
Warwick, RI 02888
(401) 463-0202 (Voice/TTY)
(800) 916-TECH (RI)
E-mail: techaccess@techaccess-ri.org
Paula Olivieri

TENNESSEE

East Tennessee Technology Access Center, Inc.
4918 North Broadway
Knoxville, TN 37918
(423) 219-0130 (Voice/TTY)
E-mail: etstactn@aol.com
WWW: *http://www.korrnet.org/ettac/*
Lois Symington

Mid-South Access Center for Technology
University of Memphis
College of Education
Ball Hall Rm.307B
Memphis, TN 38152
(901) 678-3919
E-mail: kanderso@memphis.edu
WWW: *http://www.people.memphis.edu/~coe_act/*
Karen Anderson

Signal Center's Assistive Technology Center
109 North Germantown Road
Chattanooga, TN 37411
(423) 698-8528 x200
E-mail: littleton@signal.chattanooga.net
Molly Littleton

Technology Access Center of Middle Tennessee
Fountain Square, Suite 126
2222 Metrocenter Blvd.
Nashville, TN 37228
(615) 248-6733 (Voice/TTY)
(800) 368-4651
Email: techaccess@mindstate.com
WWW: *http://tac.ataccess.org*
Bob Kibler

West Tennessee Special Technology Access Resource Center (STAR)
60 Lynoak Cove Jackson, TN 38305
(901) 668-3888
(800) 464-5619
E-mail: infostar@starcenter.tn.org
WWW: *http://www.starcenter.tn.org*
Margaret Doumitt

UTAH

The Computer Center for Citizens with Disabilities
c/o Utah Center for Assistive Technology
1595 West 500 South
Salt Lake City, UT 84104
(801) 887-9500 (Voice/TTY)
E-mail: cboogaar@usor.state.ut.us
Craig Boogaard

VIRGIN ISLANDS

Virgin Islands Resource Center for the Disabled, Inc.
P.O. Box 308427
St. Thomas, VI 00803-8427
(340) 777-2253
Email: vircd@islands.vi
Mary Ann Ramirez

VIRGINIA

Tidewater Center for Technology Access
1413 Laskin Road
Virginia Beach, VA 23451
(757) 437-6542 (Voice/TTY)
E-mail: tcta@aol.com
WWW: *http://tcta.ataccess.org*
Jane Quenneville

WEST VIRGINIA

Eastern Panhandle Technology Access Center, Inc.
P.O. Box 987
300 S. Lawrence St.
Charles Town, WV 25414
(304) 725-6473
E-mail: eptac@webcombo.net
WWW: *http://eptac.ataccess.org*
Karen Spurrier

INDEX OF SOFTWARE TITLES

SUBJECT INDEX